HARDY'S WESSEX LOCATIONS

F. P. Pitfield

Dorset Publishing Company
at the Wincanton Press, National School,
North Street, Wincanton, Somerset BA9 9AT

Also by F.P. Pitfield

The Book of Bere Regis
Dorset Parishes Churches
Purbeck Parish Churches

First published 1992. Copyright F.P. Pitfield © 1992.

Published by Dorset Publishing Company at Wincanton Press, National School, North Street, Wincanton, Somerset BA9 9AT (0963 32583).

Typeset in Bookman typeface by Bookman Limited, Merrywood Road, Bristol BS3 1DX, with typographical design by Sandra Goodman and the layout of illustrations by Rodney Legg.

Printed in Great Britain by the Alden Press, at Osney Mead, Oxford OX2 0EF.

Distributed in Dorset by Maurice Hann from 36 Langdon Road, Parkstone, Poole BH14 9EH (0202 738248).

International standard book number [ISBN] 0 948699 40 X

Illustrations in this book from the ten volumes of the three editions of John Hutchins's History and Antiquities of the County of Dorset *have been reproduced from the sets in the Rodney Legg collection. Likewise reproductions from John Pouncy's* Dorsetshire Photographically Illustrated. *Modern drawings, including those based on old photographs, are by the author, Fred Pitfield.*

Contents

TABLE OF ADDRESSES RELATED TO HARDY'S NOVELS AND SHORT STORIES

	Permanent homes and long-term lodgings	Schools, places of work, significant visits and events	General notes and works of fiction
1840–48	Higher Bockhampton	*Born 2 June 1840*	
1848–49	as above	*Village school at Lower Bockhampton*	
1849–53	as above	*British School (boys), Greyhound Yard, off South Street, Dorchester*	*Master, Isaac Glanfield Last*
1853–56	as above	*Isaac Last's Academy, Back South Street (now Charles Street), Dorchester*	*Isaac Last left the British School and set up his own academy. Hardy transferred at the same time*
1856–62	Higher Bockhampton, and latterly lodging with John Hicks and at other lodgings in Dorchester	*Architectural pupil to John Hicks at 39 South Street, Dorchester*	*July 1856–April 1862*
1862–63	3 Clarence Place, Kilburn, London	*Architectural assistant to Arthur Blomfield, at 8 St Martin's Place, London*	*A.W. Blomfield moved to new offices early in 1863*
1863–67	16 Westbourne Park Villas, Bayswater, London	*as above at 8 Adelphi Terrace, London*	*July 1867 Hardy returned to Dorset due to ill health*
1867–69	Higher Bockhampton	*Architectural assistant to John Hicks at 39 South Street, Dorchester. (John Hicks died Feb. 1869 – practice taken over by G.R. Crickmay of Weymouth)*	The Poor Man and the Lady *written 1867–68 (unpublished)*
1869–70	3 Wooperton Street, Weymouth (lodgings) and Higher Bockhampton	*Architectural assistant to G.R. Crickmay, 77, St Thomas Street, Weymouth. 7–11 March 1870, first visit to St Juliot, Cornwall*	Desperate Remedies *written*
1870 (May onwards)	Westbourne Park, London	*Part-time assistant to Arthur Blomfield at 8, Adelphi Terrace and Raphael Brandon at St Clement's Inn. 8 Aug to Cornwall*	
1871–72	3 Wooperton Street, Weymouth, Higher Bockhampton and 1 West Parade, Weymouth	*Architectural assistant to G.R. Crickmay at 77, St Thomas Street, Weymouth*	Desperate Remedies *published 25 Nov 1871. Summer 1871* Under the Greenwood Tree *written,* A Pair of Blue Eyes *begun*
1872 (March–August)	4 Celbridge Place, Westbourne Park, London	*Architectural assistant to T. Roger Smith at Bedford Chambers, London. Aug. Holiday to Cornwall – did not resume architectural career*	Under the Greenwood Tree *published 15 June 1872*
1872–74	Higher Bockhampton	*June 1873, holiday to London, Cambridge and Bath. 21 Sept. 1873 to Woodbury Hill Fair. Dec. 1873 to Cornwall 17 Sept. 1874, married Emma Lavinia Gifford at Paddington.*	A Pair of Blue Eyes *serial publication Sept. 1872–July 1873: pub. complete May 1873. Summer 1873 writing* Far from the Madding Crowd. *Dec. 1873 first instalment published. July 1874 finished writing* Far from the Madding Crowd.
1874–75	St David's, Hook Road, Surbiton Oct 1874-March 1875		*Nov. 1874* Far from the Madding Crowd *published complete. Dec. 1874 started writing* The Hand of Ethelberta.
1875–76	Newton Road, Westbourne Grove, London. March 1875–July 1875		*Serial publication of* The Hand of Ethelberta *July 1875–May 1876*
	West End Cottage off Seymour Road, Swanage. July 1875–March 1876		*Jan. 1876, finished writing* The Hand of Ethelberta
	7 Peter Street, Yeovil. March 1876–July 1876	*May 1876 holiday to Holland and The Rhine*	*Apr. 1876,* The Hand of Ethelberta *published complete*
1876–78	Riverside Villa, Sturminster Newton. July 1876–March 1878	*The Hardy's first real home. Their stay here was their "happiest time".*	The Return of the Native *written 1877–78, serial publication Feb. 1878–Jan. 1879*

1878–81	The Larches, 1, Arundel Terrace, Trinity Road, Upper Tooting, London. March 1878–June 18881	*Feb. and Aug. 1879 working holidays in Dorset researching for* The Trumpet Major. *Aug. 1880 holiday to Normandy and Cambridge. Oct 1880–Apr. 1881 confined to bed with serious illness*	*Nov. 1878,* The Return of the Native *published complete. 1878* An Indiscretion in the Life of an Heiress. *Apr. 1879* The Distracted Preacher *Apr. 1880* Fellow Townsmen. The Trumpet Major *written 1879–80, serial publ. Jan–Dec 1880, publ. complete Oct 1880.* A Laodiceau *written 1880–81, serial publ. from Dec. 1880*
1881–83	Llanherne, The Avenue, Wimborne June 1881–June 1883	*25 June 1881, first night at Wimborne saw Tebbutt's Comet. Aug. 1881 holiday to Scotland and Lake District. Oct. 1882 holiday to Paris*	*Dec. 1881* A Laodicean *published complete. Dec. 1881* What the Shepherd Saw. *Oct. 1882* Two on a Tower *publ. complete. Dec. 1882* A Tradition of 1804. *Mar 1883* The Three Strangers. *Winter 1882–83* The Romantic Adventures of a Milkmaid *written*
1883–85	7 Shire Hall Lane, (now Glyde Path Road) Dorchester. June 1883–June 1885	*July 1883 visited William Barnes at Winterborne Came Church and Rectory. Aug. 1883 visited Jersey. Nov. 1883 building work on Max Gate begun. Aug. 1884, to the Channel Islands. Early 1885 visited Eggesford, North Devon.*	*Midsummer 1883,* The Romantic Adventures of a Milkmaid *published. Apr. 1884, began writing* The Mayor of Casterbridge *May 1884* Interlopers at The Knap. *Mar. 1885* A Tryst at an Ancient Earthwork. *Apr. 1885 finished writing* The Mayor of Casterbridge
1885	Max Gate, Wareham Road, Dorchester. Occupied 29 June 1885		*Oct. 1885,* A Mere Interlude. *Nov. 1885 began writing* The Woodlanders.
1886	as above		*Jan,* The Mayor of Casterbridge *began serial publication. May, published complete.*
1887	as above	*Mar., holiday to Italy. Apr.-Aug. in London for the season (away from Max Gate 5 months)*	*Feb. finished writing* The Woodlanders, *Mar., published complete.* Alicia's Diary *(after Italian holiday). Autumn,* The Waiting Supper.
1888	as above	*15 Sept., visited White Horse, Maiden Newton 30 Sept., visited Evershot and district*	*Jan.,* The Withered Arm. *May,* Wessex Tales *(a collection of previously published short stories) Dec.* A Tragedy of Two Ambitions.
1889	as above		*July, began writing* Tess of the d'Urbervilles. *Oct.,* The Melancholy Hussar
1890	as above		*Latter part of year adapting* Tess of the d'Urbervilles *for serial publication*
1891	as above	*Jan., to ball at Frampton Court*	*Mar.* For Conscience Sake *Mar.-June,* A Few Crusted Characters. *May* A Group of Noble Dames. *June,* To Please His Wife. *July–Dec. serial publ. of* Tess of the d'Urbervilles, *Nov., published compelte Autumn,* On the Western Circuit. *Dec.,* The Son's Veto
1892	as above	*20 July, death of Hardy's father. Oct., to Great Fawley, Berkshire*	The Pursuit of the Well-Beloved *published serially from Oct.*
1893	as above	*May, visited Ireland. June, visited Oxford. 14 Sept., tea at Frampton Court*	The Fiddler of the Reels *Spring,* Master John Horseleigh, Knight. Jude the Obscure *written 1893–94*
1894	as above		*Feb.,* Life's Little Ironics, *a collection of previously published short stories. Apr.,* An Imaginative Woman. *Dec., serial publication of* Jude the Obscure *began*

1895	**Max Gate**		*1 Nov.* Jude the Obscure *published complete*
1896	**as above**		*Nov.,* A Committee Man of the Terror. *Dec.* The Duke's Re-appearance
1897	**as above**		*Mar.* The Well-Beloved *published complete. Dec.* The Grave by the Handpost
1900	**as above**		Enter a Dragoon *and* A Changed Man.
1904	**as above**	*3 April, death of Hardy's mother*	
1910	**as above**	*Received O.M. and freedom of Dorchester*	
1912	**as above**	*27 Nov. death of Hardy's wife Emma*	
1913	**as above**		A Changed Man and Other Tales, *a collection of previously published short stories*
1914	**as above**	*10 Feb. married Florence Emily Dugdale*	
1920	**as above**	*9 Feb. received honorary D. Litt at Oxford University*	
1928	**as above**	*11 Jan. Hardy died at Max Gate, Dorchester*	
1928	**Ashes buried in Poet's Corner, Westminster Abbey; heart at Stinsford churchyard, Dorset**	*14 Jan., cremation at Woking, with 15 Jan. funeral service in Westminster Abbey*	
1929			*Feb.,* Old Mrs. Chundle *published posthumously (written c. 1888–90)*

Changing face of Thomas Hardy (1840–1928) who would shave off his beard for old age. From the Strand Magazine in a tribute of 1891 to the novelist at the height of his fame. He is seen at ages 21, 32, 40 and 50. Source: Rodney Legg collection.

Table of Addresses

Introduction

SO MUCH has been written on the life and works of Thomas Hardy (1840–1928), that it is only intended here to deal with those aspects which are relevant to the locations which form the settings for his novels and short stories. More than any other writer, Hardy made use of real buildings, features and places which were given fictitious names, often more apt or descriptive than the real ones, and this was to prove one of the most popular aspects of his work. At a time when tourism was beginning to become common, many readers eagerly set out to explore the "Wessex" area with a view to identifying and discovering the real places behind the fictitious names, and guide books to cater for this need soon began to appear.

First in the field was *The Hardy Country* by C.G. Harper (1904), closely followed by *The Wessex of Thomas Hardy* by B.C.A. Windle (1906), both illustrated by line drawings, but the most authoritative work on the subject was *Thomas Hardy's Wessex* by Hermann Lea (1913), illustrated by the author's own photographs. As a personal friend of Hardy, Lea had the advantage of the author's collaboration on the project, and they travelled around the region together, by bicycle or car, visiting many of the locations referred to. Thus, Lea's work must still be regarded as the most authoritative, although in many cases positive identifications seem to have been deliberately avoided in order to prevent any possible offence or inconvenience to the occupiers of houses or cottages, and in other cases, where the locations or fictional episodes were considered of lesser importance, these seem often to have been either ignored or perhaps overlooked. In addition, Hardy's memory was understandably not always entirely reliable, particularly concerning earlier works written some twenty or thirty years previously. More recent books on the subject have included *A Hardy Companion* by F.B. Pinion (1968) and *Hardy's Wessex Reappraised* by Denys Kay-Robinson (1972) besides a great number of booklets and pamphlets.

The varied nature of the countryside in the immediate vicinity of Higher Bockhampton, where Hardy was born and spent his formative years, must have been one of the most influential factors in his later career as a writer. Dorset has a great variety of underlying geological formations producing an extremely varied landscape within its boundaries, and nowhere is this more evident than at Higher Bockhampton which is at the junction of several regions of differing landscape character. Virtually from his doorstep, Hardy could see the heathland extending away eastwards, the chalk downlands to the west and north, the woodlands of Yellowham nearby, and immediately to the south the wide alluvial valley of the Frome. In addition, town life was represented in the nearby county town of Dorchester and the fashionable seaside resort of Weymouth. Thus, most of the ingredients which Hardy was to make use of in the descriptive parts of his writings lay immediately to hand.

Hardy's early training as an architect also exercised a considerable influence on his writing; not only do buildings play an important part in his narratives, but they are described with an architect's eye to detail. Also, architects figure as characters in three of his first eight novels, showing Hardy's obvious familiarity with the workings of an architectural practice. His career in architecture between 1856 and 1872 was at a time when Victorian church restorations were at their height, and his inevitable involvement in them, often resulting in the destruction of ancient architectural features, was later much regretted, and in his writing, opportunities of commenting upon the destructive nature of such restorations were seldom missed, even in cases where Hardy is known to have been involved personally. His architectural work also entailed visiting parts of the county which he might not otherwise have been familiar with, and one, more distant, commission, the restoration of Saint Juliot church in Cornwall, was to have the most profound effect on his life. There Hardy met his first wife Emma, and this romantic episode set against the dramatic scenery of the north Cornish coast, so different from his native Dorset, provided the inspiration for his third published novel, *A Pair of Blue Eyes*.

Another major factor in Hardy's work was his interest in, and knowledge of, local history and traditions, reflected in his membership of the Dorset Natural History and Antiquarian Field Club, then a somewhat more elitist society than now, from 1880 until 1893. Most of his historical material is derived from Hutchins' *History and Antiquities of the County of Dorset*, that bible of all students of Dorset history, written by John Hutchins, M.A., (1698–1773), rector of Holy Trinity, Wareham, and published in two volumes in 1774.

The most widely referred to version is the third edition, revised, updated and edited by William Shipp and James Whitworth Hodson, in four volumes published in 1861, 1863, 1868 and 1870, and consequently the most up-to-date source of reference on Dorset history when Hardy was embarking upon his literary career. Hardy's own set of the third edition is still preserved in his reconstructed study in the Dorset County Museum at Dorchester. In several cases where Hardy quotes from old documents, it is evident that the wording is taken from transcriptions in Hutchins rather than from the original sources, as any errors or omissions in the published transcriptions are reproduced in Hardy's texts. A notable example of this occurs in the short story *Master John Horseleigh, Knight*, where the whole story, including the title, is based in error upon an omission in Hutchins.

The third edition of Hutchins includes many fine contemporary engravings together with other older ones reproduced from earlier editions, and Hardy would certainly have referred to them when writing about any subject so illustrated. In fact, in many instances, in days when travelling was more difficult and time-consuming, he is likely to have relied heavily on this source rather than revisiting the actual scenes, so that a description may often be of a building as depicted in an engraving rather than of the building itself. Engravings from Hutchins and elsewhere would have been relied upon entirely in cases where buildings or other features had disappeared before Hardy's own lifetime.

In many instances the novels and short stories are set in a period some years previous to the time of writing, and this is an important factor in determining how buildings or other features may have formerly appeared, of particular relevance when considering old engravings. Sometimes, an approximate period in which the story is set is given in the preface or text, and when it is not, it is often possible to establish the period from references to datable national or local events such as the opening of a particular section of railway line. At the same time it needs to be recognised that, just as geographical regions are sometimes condensed or otherwise altered to suit the plot, so historical contexts are sometimes adapted, such as in *The Trumpet Major* which is set in the years 1804-06 and includes real events which occurred in 1789 and 1808.

In the following pages each novel and short story is considered separately in the chronological sequence in which it was written, or in some cases published, so that the development of Hardy's system of fictional place-names can be more readily appreciated and related to each particular work. In addition, fact and fiction, which can sometimes become confused, are kept entirely separate from one another; after some general introductory matter under each heading, the remainder of the text is arranged in two columns, with fictional references on the left, and factual information concerning each location opposite in the right hand column. One of the aims of this systematic arrangement is the avoidance of statements to the effect that a fictional building or location is a factual one, or that a fictional character was born or died in a real place. (A surprising number of visitors to Bere Regis church are disappointed at not being able to find the spot where Tess was buried!)

Hardy was, after all, writing fiction and not guide books, so that there are seldom any exact parallels between his fictional descriptions and the real features upon which they were based – whole geographical regions are sometimes condensed or expanded, buildings are transposed from one place to another, and in some cases buildings or places are an amalgamation of two or more.

Space does not permit the inclusion of an illustration for each location, so that those included are confined to engravings and other prints which Hardy could have referred to, particularly when they are nearly contemporary with the date of the story, supplemented by modern drawings or photographs of locations, buildings and other features not previously identified or published in this context.

The former Castle Inn in Middle Street, Yeovil, Somerset, demolished in the 1920s in connection with street widening works. It was of mediaeval origin, and features in the short story A Tragedy of Two Ambitions (see Section 25, page 61). Drawing based on an old photograph.

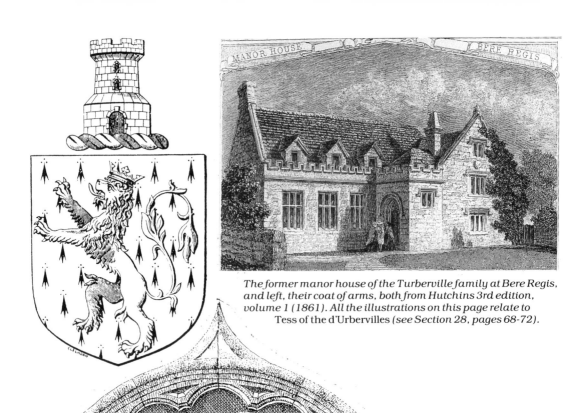

The former manor house of the Turberville family at Bere Regis, and left, their coat of arms, both from Hutchins 3rd edition, volume 1 (1861). All the illustrations on this page relate to Tess of the d'Urbervilles (see Section 28, pages 68-72).

A 14th century tomb recess of a member of the Turberville family in the south aisle of Bere Regis church.

OSTIUM SEPULCHRI ANTIQUÆ FAMILIÆ TURBERVILLE 24 JUNII 1710

THE DOOR OF THE SEPULCHRE OF THE ANCIENT FAMILY OF THE TURBERVILLES

The floor slab of the Turberville vault in the south aisle of Bere Regis church.

1. Desperate Remedies

THIS, HARDY'S first published novel, was written in 1869–70, before his familiar pattern of fictional Wessex place names had become established. At the same time, most of the places and features referred to are based on factual ones, and in the 1896 edition most of the fictional names were amended to conform to the other Wessex novels. It is therefore significant that the name of the fictional village of Carriford was not changed. As Knapwater House is based on Kingston Maurward House, the associated village of Carriford can hardly be other than Stinsford/Bockhampton, at least in a geographical sense. However, the descriptions of Carriford, its church, two inns, and nearby railway station, do not tally in any way with Stinsford and Bockhampton which are referred to collectively as Mellstock in all subsequent works.

The period of *Desperate Remedies* is the most firmly dated of all Hardy's novels – in fact each chapter heading is a date. Apart from an introductory section covering the periods 1835-36 and 1843-61, the main part of the story is set in 1864-66 and centred mostly on Budmouth-Regis and Knapwater House.

Owen Graye and his sister Cytherea leave the Midlands and arrive at Budmouth station.

Weymouth station was opened in January 1857 upon completion of the Yeovil to Weymouth line.

Owen Graye takes up a post as junior architectural assistant to Mr Gradfield, a Budmouth architect.

From 1869 to 1872 Hardy was employed as an architectural assistant by G. R. Crickmay whose office was then at 77 St Thomas Street, Weymouth.

Owen and Cytherea have their lodgings in Budmouth at 3 Cross Street.

During 1869–70 Hardy's lodgings at Weymouth were at 3 Wooperton Street. (Part of this novel was written at that time.)

Owen and Cytherea go on a paddle steamer trip to Lulwind Cove.

Lulworth Cove, Dorset's unique, almost perfectly circular coastal feature.

Whilst at Lulwind Cove, Owen takes the opportunity of walking across country to Corvsgate Castle.

Corfe Castle is a spectacular Dorset ruin dating from Norman times. It was blown up in 1646.

Owen returns to Budmouth by train from Anglebury station.

Wareham station, opened in 1847, was rebuilt in 1886.

Edward Springrove accompanies Cytherea on the return trip from Lulwind Cove to Budmouth Harbour.

Weymouth harbour was still a relatively busy port in the 19th century. Dorset's paddle steamers were based there

After taking Cytherea home, Edward "crossed the harbour-bridge, and entered his own solitary chamber on the other side".

The old harbour bridge at Weymouth, of stone with an iron swinging central section, was built in 1824 and replaced by the present bridge in 1930.

On a July evening Owen and Cytherea meet Edward Springrove on Budworth Parade.

Edward and Cytherea go rowing in the bay, past Creston Shore and as far as Ringsworth Shore.

Cytherea is interviewed by Miss Aldclyffe of Knapwater House at the Belvedere Hotel on Budmouth Esplanade.

The coach taking Cytherea to Knapwater House passed "along the Turnpike road for a distance of about a mile . . . and then turned through large lodge-gates, on the heavy stone piers of which stood a pair of bitterns cast in bronze".

In Knapwater Park Cytherea is told "that's the old manor-house – or what's left of it. . . 'Tis now divided into three cottages."

Cytherea is told that the noise of a nearby waterfall is the chief disadvantage of the old manor house.

Cytherea arrives at Knapwater House on 8 August 1864, and takes up her appointment as lady's maid and companion to Miss Aldclyffe.

Adelaide Hinton, Edward Springrove's official fiancée lives at Peakhill Cottage near Knapwater Park.

Near Knapwater House there is "a summer-house called the Fane, built . . . in the form of a Grecian temple; it overlooked the lake".

Owen Graye is sent to Tolchurch where he is to superintend the restoration of the church.

Whilst working at Tolchurch, Owen and Cytherea take up residence in part of a farmhouse near the church.

Owen Graye visits the offices of the Casterbridge Chronicle to consult a reporter's notebook.

Weymouth esplanade. During the 19th Century Weymouth still enjoyed much of its former Georgian reputation.

Preston Beach, and Ringstead Bay, the latter being almost five miles east of Weymouth.

Belvidere, on the esplanade at Weymouth, is a terrace built between 1820 and 1855. By the 1860s many of the houses had become boarding houses.

An entrance gateway still remains where a former drive to Stinsford branched off the main road (now the B3150) about a mile east of Dorchester. Until relatively recent years the piers were topped by large heraldic bird figures.

Kingston Maurward old manor house is a fine Elizabethan building which after 1720 became a farmhouse and subsequently farm cottages. Its restoration was completed in 1968.

A waterfall still remains at Kingston Maurward and takes the overflow from the east end of the lake.

Kingston Maurward House was built in 1717–20, initially in brick, but it was remodelled and faced with ashlar stone in 1794. It now forms part of the Dorset College of Agriculture.

Manor Gardens Cottage stands on a hill at the north end of Lower Bockhampton, just to the east of Kingston Maurward.

A small stone-built summer-house still stands by the lake at Kingston Maurward. Hardy included a sketch plan of it in his architectural notebook.

Tolpuddle church, of Norman origin, was restored in 1855, when the architect was T. H. Wyatt.

Tolpuddle manor house, built in 1656 stands just to the south-east of the church.

The Dorset County Chronicle office was at 58 High West Street, Dorchester, next to the Shire Hall. The street frontage remains virtually unaltered.

Anne Seaway is arrested and taken to the police station in the county town of Casterbridge.

The County Police Station in Weymouth Avenue, Dorchester, was built in 1860. The road frontage remains unaltered.

On market day, the farmers at the corn exchange of the county town talk about the Manston affair at Knapwater.

The Corn Exchange, Dorchester, was built in 1847-48 on the site of an earlier town hall. The clock turret was added in 1863.

Manston, wanted for murder, is almost captured in Mary Street, Budmouth.

St Mary Street, Weymouth, is one of the principal streets of the town.

Manston has been found hanged in his cell, and Edward Springrove watches as his coffin is carried through the prison archway.

The archway of the old county prison of 1790–92 still remains, having been retained and incorporated into the rebuilding of 1884–85.

An engraving of Corfe Castle by J.H. Le Keux from Hutchins 3rd edition, volume 1 (1861).

An engraving of Kingston Maurward House by J.H. Le Keux from Hutchins 3rd edition, volume 2 (1863). In Desperate Remedies the events at 'Knapwater House' take place in 1864-66.

Desperate Remedies

2.   Under the Greenwood Tree

THIS CHARMING and lighthearted novel is an idyllic portrayal of English rural life in the mid-19th century, featuring the Mellstock quire, a group of rustic instrumentalists and singers who were about to be phased out and replaced by a more refined and dignified organ. During the 18th and early 19th centuries there was a church band in almost every village, made up of string players, woodwind or a combination of both, and in most cases the players and singers were accommodated on a gallery at the back of the church. At Stinsford, the band was in the stringed tradition, and Hardy himself recorded the positions of the former musicians as they were in his grandfather's time, about 1835, on a gallery plan which still hangs in the church. The four players were:-

> Treble – James Hardy (JH) violin
> Counter – James Dart (JD) violin
> Tenor – Thomas Hardy junior (TH jun) violin
> Bass – Thomas Hardy senior (TH sen) violincello

The two Thomas Hardy's were Hardy's father (1811-92) and his grandfather (1778-1837), James Hardy being his uncle, so that there are obvious parallels between the real Hardys of the Stinsford band and the fictional Dewys of the Mellstock quire, in which Grandfather Dewy plays the 'cello and Reuben Dewy (Dick's father) the tenor violin.

The demise of the old choirs and church bands usually coincided with Victorian restorations which invariably involved the renewal of interior fittings and removal of the old galleries. At Stinsford, the church was restored in 1868, the architect being John Hicks of Dorchester (for whom Hardy worked as a pupil and assistant 1856–62 and 1867–69). From the report in the Dorset County Chronicle of 27 August 1868 it is evident that, unusually, the gallery was allowed to remain – "Under the tower is a gallery, which is now to be appropriated by the school children, the rear being still set apart for the singers." The work had also included the addition of a small vestry and organ chamber on the north side of the chancel. Before the 1868 restoration the organ had been situated on the gallery and surprisingly was a barrel-organ – "There are few who would pine to lose the antiquated barrel-organ which is still used in leading the musical portions of the services.". . . The gallery remained until 1911, when it was removed in the course of a further restoration.

From the Chronicle report it is apparent that the old church band at Stinsford had been replaced by a barrel-organ (not a manual one as related in the novel) at some time before 1868. When the Mellstock quire are performing outside the schoolhouse on Christmas night with no immediate response, it is suspected that they might be singing to an empty house "as befell us in the years thirty-nine and forty-three". The story must therefore be set at some time between c1845 and 1868, probably c1850.

The story begins on Christmas Eve when members of the quire are walking by way of Mellstock Cross and Mellstock Lane towards Upper Mellstock and Lewgate.

Bockhampton Cross and Bockhampton Lane, the northern part of which is known as Cuckoo Lane. Near the top of the hill a lane leads off to Higher Bockhampton.

Whilst waiting for other members of the quire, Dick Dewey had "been for a run round by Ewelease Stile and Hollow Hill" . . . to warm his feet.

Hollow Hill is a small rise where the road bends about a quarter mile west of Bockhampton Cross, this spot being three quarters of a mile south of Hardy's Cottage birthplace.

The quire assemble at Reuben Dewy's house at Upper Mellstock before making their annual rounds of the parish performing carols.

The Hardy family's cottage at Higher Bockhampton was built about 1800 for Hardy's grandfather, Hardy himself being born there on 2 June 1840.

Mellstock school is one of the first points of call for the quire. It is the home of Miss Fancy Day, the new young schoolmistress.

The old school and schoolhouse at Lower Bockhampton which Hardy attended for a time. According to the Post Office Directory for 1848 it had been "lately erected".

The quire next perform to the unappreciative farmer Shiner who is a churchwarden and one of the prime movers in the bid to disband the old quire.

A house at the south end of Lower Bockhampton facing the Frome meadows. On the 1902 Ordnance Survey map it is shown as forming part of Lower Kingston Farm.

Continuing their rounds, the quire cross Mellstock bridge and pass along "an embowered path beside the Froom towards the church and vicarage".

Bockhampton bridge stands at the lower end of the village where a tree-lined riverside path leads to Stinsford church and the old rectory.

On reaching the church, the quire go up to the gallery where they have a late supper.

Stinsford church is of considerable interest architecturally, in addition to its Hardy associations.

After their meal the quire resume their carol singing outside Mellstock vicarage.

The Old Rectory at Stinsford is a large, mostly 18th century house just to the east of the churchyard.

Some time later, the quire hold a meeting outside the workshop of shoemaker Robert Penny. His premises were "the last house in that part of the parish and stood in a hollow by the roadside".

The last house on the east side at the lower end of Bockhampton has an outbuilding the floor of which is partly below road level.

The Keeper's Cottage in Yalbury Wood is the home of Geoffrey Day. It is the scene later of the wedding reception and dancing on the grass plot in front of it, "under the greenwood tree".

The keeper's cottage in Yellowham Wood lies in a hollow to the north of the A35, and its isolated setting has changed little since Hardy's day.

On an errand to Budmouth-Regis, Dick Dewy meets Fancy Day at the corner of Mary Street near the king's statue.

The king's statue, Weymouth, was erected in 1809 to commemorate the 50th year of King George III's reign.

Driving along Budmouth esplanade they pass "the two semicircular bays of the Old Royal Hotel" which had been patronised by King George III.

The old Royal Hotel on Weymouth esplanade was built in 1772–73 and replaced by the present building in 1897.

Dick Dewy stops at the Ship Inn, "four miles out of Budmouth", to rest his horse. Here, he and Fancy become secretly engaged.

The Ship Inn, Upwey, stands in the hamlet of Elwell on the southern slopes of Ridgeway Hill.

When Dick Dewy goes nutting in Grey's Wood, he walks there by way of a winding woodland path known as Snail Creep.

A winding woodland path still exists in the narrow wood known as 'Snail Creep' between Higher Bockhampton and Cuckoo Corner. Grey's Wood lies to the north of the A35.

Dick attends the funeral of a friend at Charmley.

Charminster lies about three miles from Bockhampton, along a direct route via Frome Whitfield.

Dick Dewy and Parson Maybold walk together from Mellstock to Casterbridge, as far as Grey's Bridge.

Grey's Bridge, Dorchester was built in 1748, in association with the newly constructed London Road.

After parting from Parson Maybold at Grey's Bridge, Dick continues in the direction of Durnover Mill.

Much of the former Fordington Mill still remains, having been converted into flats during the 1930s.

From the keeper's cottage in Yalbury Wood the wedding party "threaded their way into the high road over Yalbury Hill, which dipped at that point directly into the village of Geoffrey Day's parish", where the wedding ceremony took place.

The old road over Yellowham Hill lies slightly to the south of the present A35, the track of which is still clearly marked. The keeper's cottage lies within the parish of Puddletown. Roadworks of 1991–92 pass just to the south of the original road on the western slope.

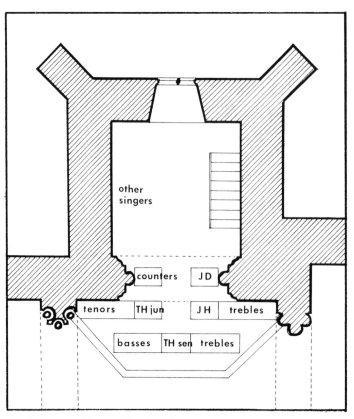

The seating arrangement of the players and singers on the former west gallery at Stinsford church, circa 1835, as recorded on Hardy's plan which hangs in the church.

TH sen. – Thomas Hardy (1778-1837) – Bass (violoncello)
TH jun. – Thomas Hardy (1811-1892) – Tenor (violin)
JH   – James Hardy (1805-188-) – Treble (violin)
JD   – James Dart (181--187-) – Counter (violin)

3.   A Pair of Blue Eyes

PERHAPS ALL of Hardy's novels could be regarded as autobiographical to some extent insofar as they are usually set in real places he knew well, and feature characters many of whom were probably drawn from real life. *A Pair of Blue Eyes* is distinctly autobiographical, the story being woven around a real and formative episode in Hardy's own life. After the death of his employer John Hicks of Dorchester in 1869, the architectural practice was taken over by G R Crickmay of Weymouth who persuaded Hardy to remain under the new management in order to ensure more effective continuity for current building projects, particularly in the case of church restorations. Most of these were in Dorset, but in 1870 Hardy was sent to north Cornwall to survey the church of St Juliot near Boscastle, leading to a restoration in 1872, and here he first met the rector's sister-in-law Emma Lavinia Gifford, which led to their marriage in 1874.

Undoubtedly the heroine Elfride Swancourt is based on Emma, and the young architect working on the restoration of Endelstow church, Stephen Smith, must be based on Hardy himself, particularly as Smith's father, like Hardy's, was a master mason. On the other hand, Stephen Smith's friend and rival in love, Henry Knight, is a writer, and this may perhaps be seen as a dual characterisation of Hardy at a time when he was considering giving up architecture as a career in favour of writing.

Stephen Smith stays with the rector and his daughter Elfride at West Endelstow Rectory whilst surveying the church.

Thomas Hardy stayed with the rector and his sister-in-law Emma at St Juliot Rectory whilst surveying St Juliot church. The old rectory is situated almost half a mile to the north west of the church.

Stephen Smith, acting on behalf of his employer, Mr Hewby, surveys West Endelstow church and later superintends the restoration works which include demolition and rebuilding of the tower.

St Juliot church was restored in 1871-72 under Hardy's direction on behalf of his employer Crickway. It was a typical Cornish church, and Hardy included a sketch of its original plan form in his architectural notebook with the note – "N.B. The old nave was rebuilt as an aisle – & the old south aisle made the nave – the Transept being pulled down." The tower also was rebuilt.

Elfride, her father and Stephen visit Endelstow House, the home of Lord Luxellian and his family.

Lanhydrock House near Bodmin lies some seventeen miles south of Boscastle. It was built in the 17th century, but was largely destroyed by fire in 1881, and was afterwards rebuilt in its original form.

Stephen and Elfride walk by the cliffs beyond Targan Bay as far as one known as "Windy Beak".

Cambeak is a prominent headland beyond The Strangles some four miles up the coast from Boscastle.

Elfride rides to St Launce's to catch the train to Plymouth.

Launceston is an ancient market town which was formerly the county town of Cornwall.

Elfride arrives at St Launce's, "and going down the hill she entered the courtyard of the Falcon".

The White Hart, Launceston has a Norman doorway which is said to have come from a local abbey.

Elfride and Stephen return by train to St Launce's after their abandoned elopement to London via Plymouth.

The railway reached Launceston in 1865, the line being opened for passenger traffic on 1 July.

The Reverend and Mrs Swancourt, Elfride and Henry Knight drive to Barwith Strand where they picnic on the beach.

Trebarwith Strand is a large beach about four miles down the coast from Boscastle.

Elfride goes to the cliffs to watch for the steamboat sailing from Bristol to Castle Boterel. She walks beside a brook as far as the cliff edge – "The small stream here found its death. Running over the precipice it was dispersed in spray before it was halfway down". . .

At Pentargan Bay, a small inlet north east of Boscastle, a little stream ends abruptly in a cascade over the cliff edge.

Elfride and Henry Knight walk to the top of "the Cliff without a Name" where Henry is dramatically saved from falling to his death by Elfride. "The crest of this terrible natural facade passed among the neighbouring inhabitants as being seven hundred feet above the water it overhung."

High Cliff, some two miles up the coast from Pentargon Bay, at 223 metres (731 feet) above sea level, is the highest cliff on the north Cornish coast, and one of the highest in England.

Stephen Smith, having returned from abroad, takes the steamboat from Bristol and lands at Castle Boterel quay.

The harbour at Boscastle is a unique tidal inlet, partly natural and partly man-made.

Stephen leaves his luggage at the local inn at Castle Boterel before walking to East Endelstow.

The former Ship Inn in Valency Road Boscastle is now a private house, but a ship medallion still remains above the doorway.

Lady Luxellian has died and her body is buried in the family vault beneath East Endelstow church.

Lesnewth church lies about half a mile south of St Juliot's on the opposite side of the Valency valley.

Elfride and Henry Knight walk along the valley near her home.

The Valency valley forms a beautiful setting for the river Valency which babbles its way to the sea at Boscastle.

Elfride visits widow Jethway's cottage which was situated "some way down the valley", and "stood absolutely alone".

A lonely stone cottage stands on the slopes of the valley about half a mile west of St Juliot church.

Stephen Smith's mother "used to go looking for owls' feathers" in the ruins of St Launce's castle.

The ruins of the Norman castle dominate Launceston. During the 13th century it was the chief castle of the Earls of Cornwall.

Mrs Smith, on her way to the market in St Launce's, was greeted by a young lawyer "in the very front of the Town Hall".

The Town Hall at Launceston is a 19th century building which replaced the old town hall demolished in 1840.

Young Mr Werrington of St Launce's is "the man in Hill Street, who plays and sells flutes, and fiddles, and grand pianners".

Stephen Smith and Henry Knight, travelling by train from London, arrive at Camelton station.

Near the parish church in Launceston there is a fine old shop front across the end of the block between High Street and Church Street. It is now a florist's but is said to have been a music shop in former days.

Hardy seems to have indulged in a little prophecy here, for the North Cornwall Railway (later part of the LSWR network) from Launceston to Wadebridge was built in stages between 1886 and 1895, reaching Camelford in 1893, twenty years after this novel was completed.

St. Juliot Old Rectory, Cornwall.

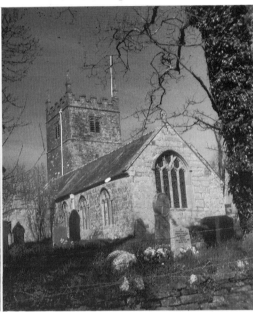

St. Juliot church, Cornwall.

An isolated cottage on the slopes of the Valency Valley west of St. Juliot church, Cornwall.

4. Far from the Madding Crowd

HARDY'S REPUTATION as a novelist became firmly established upon the publication of this novel in 1874, and it still remains one of his most popular. It is set mainly in and around Weatherbury (Puddletown), a village Hardy knew well, as several of his relatives lived there. No particular date for the story is suggested either in the preface or the text, so that c1873, when it was written, is generally assumed. However, several references suggest that Hardy may have had an earlier date in mind – in chapter 12 the Casterbridge corn exchange is described as a "low though extensive hall, supported by beams and pillars", and in chapter 48 William Boldwood is described as standing "under the portico of the old corn exchange", both suggesting that Hardy was referring to the earlier building which was replaced by the present one in 1848. Also, in chapter 56, the Weatherbury choir are said to be learning a new hymn, *Lead, Kindly Light* which was written by Cardinal Newman in 1834, although it may well have been new to the Weatherbury choir some years after its first appearance.

Most of the buildings and other features referred to still remain and are readily identifiable, except the old malthouse which was demolished in the 1870s. Other buildings have sometimes a differing fictional location, notably Weatherbury Upper Farm (Waterston House) which is imagined to have been much closer to the village than it is in fact. "Norcombe Hill" which features in the opening scenes as the site of Gabriel Oak's sheep farm is described as "not far from lonely Toller-Down", although Hermann Lea considered it to represent Toller Down itself. Between Toller Whelme and Hooke, Westcombe Coppice is situated on a spur of Toller Down, and only a substitution of compass points is required to convert *West*combe into *Nor*combe, and moreover it fits Hardy's description of the hill being half bare and half wooded.

Gabriel Oak's sheep farm is situated on Norcombe Hill. Here he first meets Bathsheba Everdene who is staying at her aunts' cottage nearby.

Westcombe Coppice covers part of a spur of Toller Down between Toller Whelme and Hooke.

Bathsheba rides through the plantation on Norcombe Hill on an errand for her aunt to Tewnell Mill.

The old mill-house at Hooke lies three-quarters of a mile south of Westcombe Coppice.

After the tragic loss of his sheep Gabriel Oak goes to the annual hiring fair at Casterbridge in search of a post as farm bailiff or shepherd.

The Dorchester Candlemas or hiring fair was held annually in February in the market place adjoining the old corn exchange.

Bathsheba Everdene has inherited Weatherbury Upper Farm after the death of her uncle, and so becomes mistress of the house and farm.

Waterston House, upstream from Puddletown, is of 17th century origin incorporating a stone frontispiece of 1586. It was considerably damaged by fire in 1863 and largely rebuilt in the following year.

The 11th Dragoon Guards were stationed at Casterbridge barracks before being posted further up country, and Fanny Robin, a servant girl of Bathsheba's is believed to have followed them.

The old Artillery barracks on the east side of Poundbury Road, Dorchester, known as the Marabout Barracks, were built in 1794–95. (The infantry barracks off Bridport Road were not built until the late 1870s.)

William Boldwood, a much respected bachelor and farmer, is the tenant of Little Weatherbury Farm, adjoining Bathsheba's.

Druce Farm lies in the Piddle Valley about a mile north west of Puddletown.

At Weatherbury Upper Farm, "The sheep-washing pool was a perfectly circular basin of brickwork in the meadows, full of the clearest water."

The old sheep-dip at Waterston survived until relatively recent years. A few broken bricks are all that now remain to mark the site.

Gabriel Oak lived near Weatherbury Upper Farm "Across the valley at Nest Cottage", which appeared "as a white spot on the opposite hill, backed by blue firs".

A former cottage which stood near a bend in the road at Chine Hill between Druce and Waterston appears on the 1902 Ordnance Survey map.

In June the great barn at Weatherbury Upper Farm was cleared out and used for the sheep shearing. In plan it "resembled a church with transepts". . .

Based on one of the Dorset monastic tithe barns such as that at Abbotsbury which dates from c1400. It is some 150 feet long and was originally almost twice that length.

Sergeant Troy was born at Weatherbury and educated at Casterbridge Grammar School. The locals believed that he "Learnt all languages while he was there, and . . . he could take down Chinese in shorthand;". . .

Dorchester Grammar School was founded in 1569 by Thomas Hardye, and the original building in South Street was rebuilt on the same site in 1883. It was moved to its present site off South Court Avenue in 1927, the foundation stone of the new building being laid by Thomas Hardy O.M. It is now known as Hardye's School.

Oak and Coggan follow the tracks of Bathsheba's horse and trap, believing them to have been stolen by gipsies. When they finally catch up with them at Sherton turnpike it proves to be Bathsheba herself making a clandestine journey to Bath.

West Hill Cottage is a former toll-house south of Sherborne at the junction of the Dorchester (A352) and Blandford (A3030) roads.

Cain Ball has been to Bath where he has seen their mistress, Miss Everdene, in the company of a soldier. It later transpires that Bathsheba and Sergeant Troy were secretly married there.

The beautiful city of Bath is noted not only for its Roman origins, but for its rich architectural heritage of Georgian buildings.

Only a few months after their marriage, Frank Troy displeases Bathsheba through having lost more than £100 in a month at Budmouth races.

Horse racing was very popular during the 19th century when there were several local courses. The Weymouth races were held on a course at Lodmoor.

Frank Troy and Bathsheba returning to Weatherbury, pass a poor young woman on the brow of Yalbury Hill, and Troy recognises her as Fanny Robin.

The route of the old road over the top of Yellowham Hill is still quite clearly marked, and lies a little to the south of the old A35 and north of its 1991–92 re-alignment.

Fanny Robin, in a weakened condition, reaches the milestone on Mellstock Hill, and staggers on towards Casterbridge Union House.

The Roman milestone on Stinsford Hill has recently (1988) been reset near its original position in the bank on the approach to the new bypass. Casterbridge Union House was the Dorchester Union Workhouse; the Poor Law Institution for the District.

On approaching Grey's Bridge, she drags herself along by the iron railings in her efforts to reach Casterbridge.

Iron railings still remain by the roadside on the approach to Grey's Bridge on the eastern side of Dorchester.

In order to avoid passing through the town itself, Fanny "turned to the left into the dense shade of a deserted avenue of chestnuts, and so skirted the borough".

Salisbury Walks is one of a series of avenues following the course of the former Roman walls around Dorchester, this section forming part of the eastern boundary.

She eventually arrives at Casterbridge Union-house in the early hours of the morning.

Damers Hospital in Damers Road Dorchester, formerly the Union Workhouse, was built in 1836.

"As the clock over the South Street Alms-house pointed to five minutes to three," Joseph Poorgrass passed by on his way to the Union-house to collect Fanny Robin's body.

"Napper's Mite" almshouse in South Street, Dorchester was built in 1616. The street frontage was rebuilt in 1842, and since 1955 the building has been used as shops and offices.

"At the roadside hamlet called Roy-Town, . . . was the old inn Buck's Head," where Joseph Poorgrass stopped for a mug of ale.

Troytown, between Puddletown and Dorchester comprises a farm and associated cottages. An old brick and cob outbuilding opposite the farm may have formed part of a former inn.

Frank Troy, after planting flowers late at night on Fanny's grave by Weatherbury church tower, sleeps on a bench in the north porch.

Puddletown church is one of the most interesting in Dorset. The tower, first built in the 12th century, was widened in the 13th century and heightened in the 15th.

Frank Troy, having left Weatherbury but still with no particular plan in mind, stops for a swim at Lulwind Cove where he is swept out to sea and presumed drowned.

Lulworth Cove, one of the most notable features on Dorset's varied coastline, is almost perfectly circular in shape. It is land-locked apart from a gap on the south side where the sea has broken through the rocks.

Bathsheba faints in Casterbridge market on being told of her husband's presumed death. She is supported by William Boldwood "who had been observing her from under the portico of the old corn exchange".

Dorchester's old corn exchange and town hall, with its archway to North Square and first floor balcony, was built in 1792. It was replaced by the present building in 1848.

William Boldwood carries the unconscious Bathsheba into the nearby King's Arms Inn where she soon recovers.

The King's Arms Hotel, Dorchester, is a fine old coaching inn with a prominent bow window above the entrance portico.

Most of the Weatherbury people attend Greenhill Fair for both business and pleasure. Here Frank Troy (who was not drowned as supposed) performed as Dick Turpin.

The sheep of Bathsheba's and Boldwood's combined flock were driven towards Greenhill fair "through the decayed old town of Kingsbere,". . .

Before returning to Weatherbury "Troy was sitting in a corner of The White Hart Tavern at Casterbridge, smoking and drinking,". . .

After shooting Frank Troy, Boldwood goes to Casterbridge gaol to give himself up. He "halted before an archway of heavy stonework, which was closed by an iron-studded pair of doors".

On an evening walk into the village, Bathsheba "reached a little shop . . . which stood nearly opposite to the churchyard".

Gabriel Oak was a member of the Weatherbury church choir, and Bathsheba could distinguish his "bass voice . . . rolling out from the gallery overhead".

Gabriel Oak visits Weatherbury vicarage to make arrangements for his marriage to Bathsheba.

The ancient annual fair on Woodbury Hill near Bere Regis was the largest in the south of England. It formerly lasted a week but by the 19th century it was a two-day event only.

Bere Regis, an ancient village which was a royal manor from Saxon times until 1259. It was formerly referred to as a town, and the name generally occurs as 'Kingsbere' in mediaeval documents.

The White Hart Hotel at the bottom of High East Street Dorchester has been almost totally rebuilt since the 19th century.

The old Dorchester prison was built on the present site in 1790–92, and the original stone entrance arch was retained when the prison was totally rebuilt in 1884–85.

The square at Puddletown has changed little since the 19th century, and the village shop with its distinctive Palladian window remains a prominent feature.

The interior of Puddletown church is remarkable for its complete 17th century fittings, which include the pulpit, box pews and west gallery dated 1635.

The old vicarage at Puddletown is a fine old building dating from the 17th and 18th centuries. It is now known as Dawnay House.

Waterston House. An engraving by J.H. Le Keux from Hutchins 3rd edition, volume 2 (1863) showing the house before being severely damaged by fire in that year.

5. The Hand of Ethelberta

HARDY'S FASCINATION with rigid Victorian class divisions and the challenging aspects of any attempts to move upwards from one category to another, is apparent in most of his plots, but the situation is exploited to the full in this light-hearted novel which is sub-titled "A Comedy in Chapters". Although some of the episodes take place in London, the Wessex scenes are set largely in Sandbourne (Bournemouth), Flychett (Lytchett Minster), Anglebury (Wareham) and the Purbeck area generally. According to the author's prefaces the novel appears to have been intended as a contemporary satire, so that it is assumed to be set in c1875, the time of writing.

The story begins at Anglebury where Ethelberta Petherwin, a young society widow and her mother-in-law are staying at the Red Lion.

The Red Lion Hotel, Wareham, dates from the 18th century and remains remarkably unchanged externally. The archway off North Street formerly led to the stables.

Ethelberta, setting out on an evening walk, pauses on a bridge before heading northwards from the town.

North Bridge, Wareham over the river Piddle, has one pointed arch of mediaeval origin, but the bridge was largely rebuilt in 1670.

Ethelberta crosses the railway and walks across the lonely heath as far as an oval shaped pond.

A pond near Great Ovens Hill lies about two miles north of Wareham. (Lea identifies this as the irregularly shaped Decoy Pond on Morden Heath, but this less remote and more nearly oval one seems more likely.)

Christopher Julian, a music teacher, lives in Sandbourne, and "passed through the blue shadow of the spire" . . . on his way to the Post Office.

Bournemouth. Little existed there until 1810, but by the end of the century it had grown into a large and fashionable resort. St Peter's, the 'Mother Church' of Bournemouth, was built by George Edmund Street in 1862 but, Rodney Legg points out, its tower was not erected until 1870 and the spire was not added to that until 1879. For years, however – since 1860 – Phillip Brannon's drawing for his *Illustrated, Historical and Picturesque Guide to Bournemouth* had shown the building as if it were already complete. In fact the spire does cast a shadow across the street and the Post Office was, and is, not far around the corner.

Christopher Julian and his sister are engaged to play music for a ball organised by Ethelberta at Wyndway House.

Upton House on the shores of Poole Harbour is a dignified Georgian house built early in the 19th century. Its grounds now form Upton Country Park.

Christopher Julian often enjoyed standing alone on Sandbourne pier on winter evenings, when the dimly seen waves making for the shore gave a sensation of outward bound movement to the pier.

The original timber pier at Bournemouth built in 1861, was weakened by ship-worms and destroyed by gales (1867–76), Rodney Legg writes. The replacement of 1878 was by the grand-master of Victorian pier-building, Eugenius Birch. It was 'broken' in 1940 to prevent its use by German invaders and replaced in 1960.

After the ball at Wyndway House, Ethelberta goes to stay at Rookington Park about three miles from Sand-bourne.

Heron Court at Hurn, near Christchurch, which, says Rodney Legg, was the home of the third Earl of Malmesbury in the 1870s. He was Disraeli's Lord Privy Seal (1874–76). This Elizabethan house was altered c1840 when a third storey was added to the main block. It has been renamed Hurn Court and is now a school.

Christopher calls on Ethelberta who is staying with her family, the Chickerels, at Arrowthorne Lodge in Upper Wessex.

Minstead Lodge in the New Forest is not far from the Rufus Stone which marks the spot where King William II was assassinated (by an arrow). Identification by Rodney Legg in his *Literary Dorset*.

Ethelberta and her family take a holiday at Knollsea, and stay at the cottage of a boatman, Captain Flower.

Durlston Cottage in Park Road Swanage adjoins the downs leading to Peveril Point.

From their holiday cottage there was a fine view across the bay, and "beyond all a curved wall of cliff, terminating in a promontory, which was flanked by tall and shining obelisks of chalk. . ."

The view from the downs across Swanage Bay has changed but little since the 19th century, with white chalk cliffs where Ballard Down abruptly meets the sea.

Ethelberta, making an undignified journey on a donkey, takes an unfrequented route to Corvsgate Castle over Nine-Barrow Down.

Nine Barrow Down forms part of the inner chalk range of the Purbeck Hills stretching from Swanage to Corfe Castle.

Ethelberta, travelling along the spine of the down could see "Far below on the right hand . . . a many armed inland sea which stretched around an island with fir-trees and gorse,". . .

The view from Nine Barrow Down is one of the most spectacular in Dorset, particularly on the north side. Spread out below is the whole of Poole Harbour, with Brownsea Island and to the left the open sea fringed by the sandy beaches of Studland Bay.

On reaching Corvsgate Castle, Ethelberta "crossed the bridge over the moat, and rode under the first archway into the outer ward".

Corfe Castle is Dorset's most imposing ruin. Although the castle was blown up by Cromwell's men in 1646, the outer gate-house and bridge remain largely intact.

Ethelberta, going to visit her aunt in Cherbourg, boards the little steamer 'Speedwell' at Knollsea Pier.

The old wooden pier at Swanage was built in 1859 and superseded by the present one in 1896. The stumps of the old pier remain.

On leaving Knollsea Pier, the 'Speedwell' first took a short easterly course "to avoid a sinister ledge of limestones jutting from the water like crocodile's teeth,". . .

Peveril Point is a headland between Swanage Bay and Durlston Bay to the south, where the upward sloping limestone beds of the outer Purbeck range disappear under the sea in a line of jagged rocks.

Lord Mountclere's yacht, also bound for Cherbourg, had rounded Old-Harry Rock on its way to Knollsea.	Old Harry Rocks are isolated sections of chalk cliff at Handfast Point between Swanage and Studland Bays.
Ethelberta is a guest of Lord Mountclere at his family seat, Enckworth Court.	Encombe House, on the coast between Kimmeridge and Worth Matravers, dating mainly from the 18th century, incorporates part of an earlier house. It was considerably re-arranged internally late in the 19th century.
Ethelberta and her sister Picotee travel by train to Melchester, leaving from Anglebury station.	Wareham Station. At the date of this story, c1875, there was no rail link to Swanage, the Wareham-Swanage branch line being opened in 1885.
Ethelberta, her sister and Lord Mountclere attend a concert at the Town-hall Melchester where Christopher Julian is one of the performers.	The Guildhall, Salisbury, was built in 1788–95 on the site of an Elizabethan Council House destroyed by fire in 1780.
Whilst in Melchester, Ethelberta and her sister stay at the 'Red Lion'.	The Red Lion Hotel in Milford Street Salisbury is of 14th century date but the street facade is of 1820–23.
Lord Mountclere stays at the 'White Hart', Melchester, "the rival hotel . . . which stood in an adjoining street".	The White Hart Hotel in St John's Street, Salisbury, is a late 18th century building with an imposing Ionic portico.
Ethelberta and Christopher "turned the corner of the short street of connection which led under an archway to the Cathedral Close,". . .	The 15th century north gateway at Salisbury stands at the end of a short street off High Street and leads into the Cathedral Close.
Christopher Julian, now organist at Melchester Cathedral, shows Ethelberta around the exterior of the building.	Salisbury is one of England's finest cathedrals and almost entirely of the 13th century. The spire was added in the 14th century.
At the beginning of the cathedral service, "peals broke forth from the organ on the black oaken mass at the junction of nave and choir,". . .	Internally, Salisbury cathedral exhibits all the grace and elegance of 13th century architecture, including Purbeck marble shafted columns.
Lord Mountclere calls at Knollsea parsonage to make arrangements for his forthcoming marriage to Ethelberta.	The Old Rectory in King's Road Swanage was built in 1667 and extended in the 18th and 19th centuries. It is now two properties, the western portion being known as Swanwic House.
Sol Chickerell and the Hon. Edgar Mountclere, travelling from Sandbourne to Knollsea pass near Havenpool.	Poole, a town which was confined mainly to an area near the harbourside until the late 19th century.
Sol and Mountclere arrive at Flychett, "a trumpery small bit of a village", where they spend the rest of the night at an inn.	Lytchett Minster, probably the 'St Peter's Finger'. The name is a corruption of the latin 'St Peter ad Vincula'.

Sol Chickerell and Edgar Mountclere arrive early at Knollsea church in an attempt to stop the marriage of Ethelberta and Lord Mountclere.

Sol and Edgar enter the church and find that the marriage had taken place just before their arrival.

Christopher Julian and Picotee wait for her brother Sol at the Castle Inn, Corvsgate.

Christopher Julian . . . "passed into the hamlet of Little Enckworth . . . and drew up at a beer house at the end".

The parish church of St Mary, Swanage, was rebuilt, with the exception of the mediaeval tower, in 1859–60, and enlarged in 1907–08.

After the rebuilding in 1860 and before the enlargement of 1907–08 Swanage church was of cruciform plan with north and south transepts, both with galleries.

The Castle Inn at Corfe Castle is of early 19th century date.

The Scott Arms stands on the corner of the street at Kingston, near Corfe Castle. Rodney Legg states that it was originally the Eldon Arms. John Scott MP was created Baron Eldon of Eldon in 1799, bought the Encombe estate in the Isle of Purbeck in 1807, and as Lord Chancellor of England became the first Earl of Eldon in 1821.

A print by Philip Brannon of the old pier at Swanage soon after its construction in 1859.
Source: Rodney Legg collection.

Below: Encombe House, in the Isle of Purbeck. An engraving by J.H. Le Keux from Hutchins 3rd edition, volume 1 (1861).

6. An Indiscretion in the Life of an Heiress

HARDY'S FIRST novel *The Poor Man and the Lady*, concerning an affair between a poor schoolmaster and the wealthy daughter of the local squire, was rejected by his publishers chiefly on the grounds of its improbability, in an age when such a violation of rigid class divisions was virtually unthinkable. At the same time one of the reviewers of the manuscript considered that the young aspiring author showed promise, and Hardy was advised to attempt a novel with a less improbable theme and a more complex plot. The result was *Desperate Remedies*, published in 1871, which included some sections from *The Poor Man and the Lady*. Further scenes were used in *Under the Greenwood Tree*, and in 1878, after Hardy's reputation as a novelist had become firmly established, most of the remainder appeared as a shortened version under the title *An Indiscretion in the Life of an Heiress*. It is set in and around Stinsford/Kingston Maurward which appears as Tollamore rather than the familiar Mellstock of subsequent works, and Weymouth has the fictional name of Melport instead of Budmouth.

The Red Lion, Winfrith, before being rebuilt after the fire of 1965. Drawing based on an Edwardian picture postcard. This building features as 'The Quiet Woman' in The Return of the Native.

Two Dorset inn signs – 'The Quiet Woman' at Halstock, and 'The Silent Woman' at Coldharbour near Wareham.

7.   The Return of the Native

OF ALL Hardy's novels this is perhaps the most evocative in terms of the Wessex scenery he portrays so graphically. The timeless character of the wild Dorset heathland is perfectly captured, although even in Hardy's day some areas had been ploughed and some planted to woodland, so that 'Egdon Heath' was not so unified as inferred in the novel. Today it has become even more fragmented and reduced in area, not only by further agricultural inroads, but also by large scale coniferous afforestation, sand and gravel extraction, and building development. Nevertheless many unspoilt areas remain and it is still possible to find tracts which retain the essential character as portrayed in the novel. Before the 19th century most of this vast area of heathland lay undisturbed, stretching continuously from Higher Bockhampton in the west, across much of south east Dorset and into the New Forest, but for the purposes of the novel 'Egdon Heath' is confined to the western portion, extending eastwards only so far as Throop Heath, the nearby village of Affpuddle being referred to as 'East Egdon'. Hardy states in his preface to the 1895 edition – "The date at which the following events are assumed to have occurred may be set down as between 1840 and 1850,". . .

The novel opens with a long and graphic description of Egdon Heath.	Black Heath lying just to the south of Hardy's birthplace still remains unspoilt and now forms part of a County-owned nature trail.
Rainbarrow figures prominently throughout the novel, and "formed the pole and axis of this heathery world".	Rainbarrows are a group of three Bronze Age round barrow burial mounds on a high point of Duddle Heath overlooking the Frome valley.
Captain Vye and his grand-daughter Eustacia live at Mistover Knap, a remote spot on the heath where the cottage is situated in an enclosure near a natural pool.	Probably Greenhill Pond in Puddletown Forest about a mile south west of Puddletown. It is now in open heathland again after recent tree felling.
Mrs Yeobright "was passing down the Anglebury Road,". . . towards the Quiet Woman Inn.	The heathland route from Dorchester to Wareham via Stinsford, Tincleton and Waddock Cross.
The Quiet Woman Inn is the setting for several important episodes, the landlord and small-holder being Damon Wildeve. According to Hardy's 1912 footnote the inn is an amalgamation of three elements; – the site that of the former Duck Inn (now Duck Farm) near Norris Mill, the building the Red Lion at Winfrith, and the sign from an inn "some miles to the north west of the present scene,". . .	The Red Lion at Winfrith, formerly thatched, was largely destroyed by fire on 13 May 1965. It was afterwards rebuilt with a tiled roof. The Quiet Woman at Halstock has a painted sign, but it does not now include the sexist couplet quoted by Hardy – 'Since the woman is quiet, let no man breed a riot'. The words do, however, appear on the sign of the Silent Woman at Coldharbour near Wareham, but this is a relatively recent renaming, as it was known as the Angel Inn before about 1930.

Thomasin and her aunt "reached the place where the hollies grew, which was in a conical pit" . . . and gathered holly for the Christmas decorations.

There are a number of natural conical pits on the heath, swallowholes created by water-suction in antiquity, the largest and best known being Culpepper's Dish south of Briantspuddle. Nearby is a smaller one, known locally as The Spoon, in which holly bushes still grow.

Blooms-End, which is referred to frequently in the novel, is the home of Mrs Yeobright.

The former farmhouse at Bhompston Farm lies near the River Frome, east of Lower Bockhampton.

Clym Yeobright and Eustacia Vye are married at East Egdon church.

Affpuddle church is of 13th century origin with a fine 15th century tower and 16th century pew ends and pulpit.

After their marriage Clym and Eustacia live in a remote cottage on the heath at Alderworth in the parish of East Egdon. Behind it is a fir-tree covered knoll known as The Devil's Bellows.

Brickyard Cottages stand about half a mile south of Briantspuddle by the side of the road to Bovington. They are now known as 'The Pines' and 'Culpepper Cottage'.

After the dance at East Egdon, Wildeve accompanies Eustacia on her way home as far as Throope Corner.

Throop Clump is at the crossroads south of Throop, but their route to Eustacia's cottage is more likely to have been by way of the crossroads south of Briantspuddle.

Damon Wildeve goes in search of a policeman – "About half a mile below Clym's secluded dwelling lay a hamlet where lived one of the two constables who preserved the peace in the parish of Alderworth,". . .

Briantspuddle is a charming and quiet village of mainly thatched cottages in the eastern part of Affpuddle parish.

Mrs Yeobright, walking on the heath in scorching weather, asks a boy "can you tell me if Rimsmoor Pond is dry this summer?".

Rimsmoor Pond on Briantspuddle Heath lies about a quarter of a mile south of Brickyard Cottages.

Eustacia and Wildeve are drowned in Shadwater Weir. It "had at its foot a large circular pool, fifty feet in diameter, into which the water flowed through ten huge hatches,". . .

There are three weirs on the Frome in this vicinity – one at Bhompston Farm, another former one near West Stafford, and the largest at Woodsford. The latter is the most likely to represent Shadwater Weir particularly as references to 'Shadwater folk' suggest a closely associated village.

Diggory Venn gives up his wandering life as a reddleman and settles down to dairy farming at Stickleford.

Tincleton is a somewhat scattered village in the Frome valley bordering the heath.

Rimsmoor Pond on Briantspuddle Heath. Much of its area is now silted up, to form a spongy moss-covered bog, but one deeper section, shown in the photograph, remains clear all the year round.

The Return of the Native

8.   The Distracted Preacher

TALES OF smuggling always have some peculiar fascination, particularly when they concern adventures of bygone days involving relatively innocuous commodities such as brandy, tobacco, tea and fine silks. Dorset, having large tracts of isolated countryside adjoining the coast, was ideally suited for these activities during the 18th and early 19th centuries when smuggling was at its height, and many local inhabitants for miles inland relied upon this illicit night work to supplement their meagre incomes. Consequently there were few who did not benefit in some way from the trade, and the revenue officers got little or no support from otherwise law-abiding villagers who mostly sympathised with the smugglers and aided and abetted them in maintaining the secrecy of their ingenious hiding places for the contraband. This, one of the Wessex Tales, is said to have been based upon real events which took place between 1825 and 1830 in and around the village of Owermoigne.

Richard Stockdale, a young Wesleyan minister, arrives in Nether Moynton and takes up lodgings with a young widow, Lizzy Newberry at her house "at the upper end of the street".

A thatched house in Church Lane, Owermoigne dates from the early 18th century and its walls are a mixture of cob, stone and brick. Church Lane was formerly the main street of the village.

Lizzy takes Mr Stockdale to the church where she removes a keg from beneath the floorboards of a lumber room under the gallery and draws off a cup of brandy as a cure for his cold.

Owermoigne parish church was rebuilt in 1882 with the exception of the mediaeval west tower. A former west gallery was removed in the course of the rebuilding work.

Lizzy, on leaving Nether Moynton, crossed the turnpike road "and got into the track for Ringsworth. Here she ascended the hill,". . .

A track from Owermoigne leads over the downs to Holworth and Ringstead Bay. The section nearest Owermoigne is now tarred. 'Ringsworth' is Ringstead.

Lizzy passed "the lonely hamlet of Holworth" on her way to Ringsworth.

Holworth is a small settlement about half way between Owermoigne and the coast.

On reaching the cliffs "Lizzy soon ascended a small mound," and lit a small fire "to burn the lugger off" a warning to the smugglers that it was not safe to land the cargo that night.

The cliff at Holworth in Ringstead Bay is composed of Kimmeridge shale, and became famous as 'the burning cliff' when spontaneous combustion began in 1826 and continued for 12 years.

Lizzy and her band of smugglers pass by Lord's Barrow on their night-time journey across the downs from Nether Moynton to Lulwind Cove.

Lord's Barrow, a Bronze Age round barrow, is situated on the ridge at the side of the road between Owermoigne and West Chaldon.

"They now arrived at a ravine which lay on the outskirts of Chaldon,". . .

The road at West Chaldon passes through a steep-sided valley.

Trudging across Chaldon Down, the smugglers "reach the crest of the hill at a lonely trackless place not far from the ancient earthwork called Round Pound".

The Round Pound is an earthwork enclosure, probably of the Iron Age, on Chaldon Down, north-west of Durdle Door.

The smugglers make their landing at Dagger's Grave, "not many hundred yards from Lulwind Cove," and scramble up the cliff by means of a rope secured to an iron bar at the top.

Man o' War Bay lies just to the east of Durdle Door, and south of Dagger's Gate on the Winfrith to West Lulworth road. The offshore rocks would have caused it to be a graveyard for ships.

The Customs officers begin their search of Nether Moynton, confident of recovering the contraband and taking it to Budmouth Custom-house before nightfall.

The Custom House on the quay at Weymouth is a fine early 19th century building.

All the carts and wagons which the Customs men commandeer have been sabotaged by the villagers, but the local blacksmith is eventually tracked down and forced to repair them.

A single storey dwelling opposite the west end of Owermoigne church was formerly the village blacksmith's shop, being marked 'Smithy' on the 1902 Ordnance map.

The smugglers in female disguise way-lay the Customs men at Warm'ell Cross, tie them to trees and recover their kegs of brandy.

Warmwell Cross west of Owermoigne is now a busy traffic roundabout, but the clump of beech trees surrounding the original crossing still survives on the central island.

The hazardous offshore rocks of Man o' War Bay at West Lulworth. Beyond, can be seen, Durdle Door, Swyre Head, Bat's Head and White Nothe. Weymouth appears on the horizon eight miles away to the west.

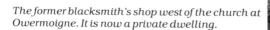

The former blacksmith's shop west of the church at Owermoigne. It is now a private dwelling.

The Distracted Preacher

9. Fellow Townsmen

THIS SHORT story, one of the *Wessex Tales*, concerns two friends and respected citizens of Port-Bredy (Bridport), and the twists of fate which affect their lives. The main part of the story takes place c1845-47, and after a lapse of more than 21 years concludes c1869 when the returning George Barnet finds that several changes have taken place in the town, most notably the arrival of the railway (1857) and a restoration and enlargement of the parish church (1859-60).

"The shepherd on the east hill could shout out lambing intelligence to the shepherd on the west hill, over the intervening town chimneys,". . .

Bridport, in spite of 19th and 20th century expansion, still lies compact between prominent hills to the east and west.

George Barnet is giving his friend Charles Downe a lift home, and they go past the town-hall.

The Town Hall, Bridport, was built in 1785–86 on the site of a former chapel.

To reach Downe's house, "Their route took them past the little town-hall, the Black-Bull Hotel, and onward to the junction of a small street on the right," . . . in which Downe's humble house was situated.

They were evidently travelling eastwards along East Street, where a right turn would have taken them into King Street, a narrow thoroughfare opening off the south side.

George Barnet is having a new house built, to be known as 'Chateau Ringdale', on the outskirts of the town by the side of the road to the harbour.

On the west side of West Bay Road, near the new Bridport bypass, there is a group of four substantial town houses which were all built in the early 1840s.

Lucy Savile (Barnet's former fiancée) lives in "one of the smallest of the detached houses by the wayside" leading to the harbour.

Lea appears to identify this as Harbour Cottage at West Bay, but this seems unlikely on geographical grounds. 74 West Bay Road, a stone and thatched cottage, would more accurately fit Hardy's description.

When Barnet took a walk, "Sometimes he went round by the lower lanes of the borough, where the rope-walks stretched,". . .

Rope making was formerly Bridport's chief industry and some of the town's side streets were specially adapted for laying out lengths of rope.

Mrs Barnet and Mrs Downe visit the harbour and take a boat trip into the bay.

Bridport's unique man-made harbour is one and a half miles south of the town at West Bay.

When the ladies' boat capsizes in a sudden squall, and both are feared drowned, a boatman is told to "go to the Harbour Inn and tell them to ride to town for a doctor".

The Bridport Arms Hotel at West Bay immediately adjoins the shingle beach. It is mostly of stone and thatch and portions date from the 17th century.

Widower Charles Downe and Lucy Savile are married at Port-Bredy church.

At this point in the story, c1847, Bridport parish church had not been restored and extended.

When George Barnet returns to Port-Bredy after an absence of more than 21 years, he finds that many changes have taken place, and "the church had had such a tremendous practical joke played upon it by some facetious restorer or other as to be scarce recognizable,". . .

George Barnet stays at the Black-Bull Hotel where he is not recognised after an absence of 21 years.

Bridport church was restored in 1859–60, involving considerable rebuilding of the east end, and extension of the nave and aisles. The architect was John Hicks of Dorchester, Hardy being at that time (1856–62) his architectural pupil and assistant who could well have prepared the drawings which are dated December 1858.

The Bull Hotel, Bridport, stands on the south side of East Street between the town hall and King Street.

The Bridport Arms Hotel beside the shingle beach at West Bay.

Below, an engraving of 1815 by Howlett from a drawing by J.C. Buckler, showing Bridport parish church before the restoration and enlargement of 1859-60. The print appears in the 2nd and 3rd editions of Hutchins.

Fellow Townsmen

10.   The Trumpet Major

THE SUMMER of 1805 must have been the greatest and most exciting season ever for Weymouth and its neighbourhood. King George the Third, the royal family and their courtiers were in residence as usual, together with a great influx of visitors drawn from 'fashionable society', and some of the best actors from the London stage were appearing at the local theatre. In addition to the ceremonial troops in their resplendent uniforms who normally attended the king and the royal family, many others had been drafted into the area, not only as an additional protection for the king but in preparation for an expected French invasion. There was also a naval presence in the bay – the battle of Trafalgar was to be fought in October 1805 – and all the patriotic fervour of the period seems to have been focussed on Weymouth and the king who was nonchalantly and defiantly taking his annual holiday as usual on the vulnerable south coast in spite of the arch enemy Bonaparte being poised for attack on the other side of the channel. This atmosphere of gaiety and patriotism set against a background of impending invasion is graphically captured in this novel which is set in and around Budmouth (Weymouth) during the years 1804–06.

Overcombe Mill is the home of miller William Loveday, part of the building being partitioned off and occupied by Widow Garland and her daughter Anne.

Although the site of the mill is Sutton Poyntz, the building itself is probably an amalgamation of Sutton Poyntz Mill, now converted to residential use, and Upwey Mill which is still in working order.

Anne Garland could see "the large, smooth mill-pond," . . . from a back window of the mill-house.

The picturesque mill-pond still remains at Sutton Poyntz just to the north of the old mill.

Oxwell Hall, "of late years used as a farmhouse", belongs to old Benjamin Derriman who ekes out a miserly and lonely existence there.

Poxwell House is a fine Elizabethan house of c1600 with an unusual brick gatehouse dated 1634. The house was restored in 1934 when the west wing was extended.

Anne Garland walks to a christening party "in the adjoining parish of Springham", beyond Oxwell Hall.

Warmwell is a small village with a basically 13th century church, just over a mile from Poxwell.

Many local people go to "the top of the Ridgeway" on a summer night to see the king's carriages pass on their way to Budmouth.

The old roadway still remains over the top of Ridgeway Hill. It followed the straight course of the Roman road and was abandoned in 1824 in favour of the present hairpin section.

From the down above Overcombe the extensive view included "the Isle, with its pebble bank, . . . like a great crouching animal tethered to the mainland".

The hills immediately north of Sutton Poyntz still afford the finest and most extensive views of Weymouth Bay and Portland.

During the king's stay in Budmouth, "a picket of a thousand men mounted guard every day in front of Gloucester Lodge, where the king resided".

Gloucester Lodge is now the Gloucester Hotel. King George III stayed there during each of his annual visits to Weymouth from 1789 until 1805.

After seeing the king and watching the changing of the guard, Trumpet-Major John Loveday and Anne Garland "went along the parade together".

Before the late 18th century Weymouth only extended northwards as far as the point where the king's statue now stands.

Whilst in Casterbridge awaiting the arrival of Matilda Johnson, Robert Loveday stays at the Old Greyhound Inn.

The Tudor archway which formed the entrance into the Old Greyhound yard off South Street, Dorchester, still remains, having been reset in the Tudor arcade which now occupies the site.

Whilst waiting for Matilda's coach to arrive at Casterbridge, Robert Loveday listens to the service taking place in All Saints Church.

All Saints Church, Dorchester, was rebuilt after the great fire of 1613 and again in 1843–45. The 17th century church would therefore have still been standing c1805.

Robert Loveday and Anne attend the afternoon service at their parish church and notice the pikes stored "in the corner of the aisle".

Preston church is of 14th, 15th and 16th century date and was restored in 1855. The pikemen's weapons were normally kept in parish churches at this time.

Bob Loveday shows Anne a cartoon he has bought in Budmouth – "It was a hieroglyphic profile of Napoleon". . .

A copy of this caricature still exists, and hangs in the County Museum at Dorchester.

Two old war veterans are now volunteers. "Instead of sitting snugly in the settle of the Old Ship, in the village adjoining Overcombe, they were obliged to keep watch on the hill".

The Ship Inn at Preston is now known as The Spice Ship.

Trumpet-Major Loveday tells Anne Garland: "We arrived at Budmouth Barracks this morning, and are to lie there all the summer."

The Red Barracks, near Hope Square Weymouth, were built in 1795 and rebuilt in 1801 after a fire. They now form part of a pleasant residential development known as Wellington Court.

Anne Garland and the Loveday brothers go to the theatre at Budmouth on a 'king's night', when the king and royal family are in attendance.

The former Theatre Royal at Weymouth was situated on the Esplanade where the Weymouth Hotel now stands.

The press-gang have their eye on a "little nest of fellows at the 'Old Rooms' in Cove Row".

The Old Rooms in Trinity Street, Weymouth, is an Elizabethan house which was used as assembly rooms during the 18th century.

Bob Loveday watches as the royal bathing machine is drawn out into the sea.

One of the bathing machines used by the king was kept at Weymouth for some time, but it is said to have ended its days as a garden shed.

On 3 September (1805) the king went out in his bathing machine, and as he entered the water, a band hidden in an adjoining machine struck up the national anthem.

This episode actually took place when King George III took his first bathe in the sea at Weymouth on 8 July 1789.

After watching the foregoing episode Bob Loveday "then passed on to the harbour", where he watched ships being loaded and unloaded.

At this period Weymouth was still a busy port handling large quantities of heavy goods.

Robert Loveday walks from Overcombe to Pos'ham to visit Captain Hardy at his home. After his personal appeal he is taken on as a crew member of the Victory.

Thomas Masterman Hardy (1760–1839) was born at Kingston Russell and lived at Portesham House before his marriage in 1807. He was captain of Nelson's flagship HMS Victory at Trafalgar, where he attended Nelson at his death.

Anne Garland, in the course of her walk to Portland, was "rowed across the Fleet (which then lacked the convenience of a bridge),". . .

The ferry across the entrance to the Fleet at Smallmouth was the usual way of reaching Portland before the first ferry-bridge was built in 1839.

Anne watches HMS Victory pass down channel towards Plymouth (and later Trafalgar) from Portland Bill where the lighthouse was the only man-made object.

The earliest lighthouses on Portland Bill, a pair, were erected in 1716. The lower one, to which Hardy refers, was reconstructed in 1789. It was 63 feet high and was rebuilt in 1869. The present lighthouse replaced it in 1905.

After leaving Portland Bill, Anne returns to Budmouth by sea, in a lerret which leaves from Hope Cove.

Church Ope Cove lies below Rufus Castle. Lerrets were rowing boats specially designed for launching off Portland's beaches.

On her way home to Overcombe, Anne "turned into a little lane" and rested near "a little spring of water, having a stone margin round it". . . Here she meets the king and his physician inspecting the well and its waters.

The medicinal property of the sulphurous water of Nottington Well was investigated by a chemist and doctors in 1719, 1749 and 1791. It became known as Nottington Spa, and the present octagonal building was erected over it in 1830.

Festus Derriman and Matilda Johnson meet in Budmouth and go to 'the Look-out'.

The Nothe, Weymouth, had been a gun emplacement since the 17th century, and the present fort was built 1860–72.

In the year after Trafalgar (i.e. in 1806) John Loveday and Anne visit the hillside where a gigantic figure of King George III on horseback is being cut.

This figure was actually cut in 1808. King George III who last visited Weymouth in 1805 could not have seen it, in spite of a local tradition that he was displeased at being depicted riding away from the town.

John Loveday and Anne Garland go for a country walk and visit the Faringdon Ruin.

A gable end of the church is all that now remains of the deserted mediaeval village of Winterbourne Farringdon.

The former Theatre Royal on the Esplanade at Weymouth. Elevational drawing compiled from old sketches.

11.   A Laodicean

"AND UNTO the angel of the church of the Laodiceans write; . . . I know thy works, that thou art neither cold nor hot. So then because thou art lukewarm. . . . I will spue thee out of my mouth." (Revelation: chapter 3, verses 14–16). Hence the title of this novel referring to the heroine Paula Power, a wealthy young heiress and owner of de Stancy Castle, who, although carrying on a family tradition of belonging to the Baptist church, is not prepared to enter into the full commitment of adult baptism. There is also an element of autobiography in this novel insofar as the other main character, George Somerset, is an architect who has studied mediaeval architecture, and whose knowledge of the subject and opinions on the restoration of ancient buildings are essentially those of Hardy himself. Also, a former architectural colleague in John Hicks's office, Henry Bastow, was an ardent Baptist, and his views are known to have had a considerable influence on Hardy.

In his general preface to the 1912 edition of the Wessex novels Hardy equates 'Toneborough' the county town, with Taunton, so that there can be no doubt that this novel is set in that region, although as is so often the case, the local topography is adapted to suit the story. Geographically de Stancy castle and its associated little town of Markton can hardly be other than Dunster as asserted by Lea, but the architectural details are evidently drawn largely from elsewhere. Much of the novel was written during a long and serious illness in 1881, being dictated to his wife Emma at his bedside, and is set in a contemporary period as the new rural Baptist chapel near Markton is described as having a plaque recording its erection in the 1870s. The plot is centred around the rebuilding and extension of the uninhabited portions of de Stancy castle, and it is perhaps significant that Dunster castle was to a large extent rebuilt and remodelled in 1868–72, the architect being Anthony Salvin.

George Somerset, a young architect studying and recording architectural details in the neighbourhood, stays at an inn in the village of Sleeping Green.

Lea considered this to refer to Withycombe or Carhampton near Dunster. At Carhampton there is an inn, The Butchers Arms.

Whilst exploring the area, Somerset unexpectedly comes across a fine old castle. It proves to be de Stancy Castle, which is owned and occupied by Paula Power, a young heiress who plans to rebuild some of the ruined parts.

Dunster Castle. A castle has stood on this site since Saxon times, but the oldest portion now surviving is a 13th century gateway. In 1617 a new building of more residential character was built and remains as the basis of the present building. It was considerably altered in 1868–72.

Markton is the little town adjoining de Stancy Castle.

Dunster is dominated by its castle. The octagonal Yarn Market was built in 1609.

The Lord Quantock Arms is the principal inn of Markton, and George Somerset stays "in this rambling edifice of stagecoach memories,". . .

The Luttrell Arms, Dunster, is a fine old inn with some portions dating from the 15th century.

Paula's father had been a railway engineer, one of his greatest works in the area being a long tunnel.

The 1092-yard-long Whiteball tunnel at Werescote, nine miles down the main line from Taunton, was designed by Brunel, and came into use in 1844.

George Somerset meets Paula at Markton church which she is visiting with her aunt, and her companion Charlotte de Stancy.

Paula is fascinated by the monuments and effigies in Markton church, commemorating the de Stancy family who had owned de Stancy Castle for centuries.

The large parish church of St George, Dunster, was formerly a priory church. Some Norman portions remain, but it is mostly of the 15th century.

There are two notable monuments with recumbent effigies of the Luttrell family in Dunster church. They owned the castle for exactly 600 years from 1376 until 1976, when it was given to the National Trust by Lieutenant-Colonel Walter Luttrell.

James Havill, a local architect and professional rival of George Somerset, has his office in High Street, Toneborough, the county town.

Taunton is the county town of Somerset. In the novel it is imagined to have been closer to 'Markton' than it is in fact.

When Paula goes away for a few weeks she leaves from Toneborough station, "there being no train from the nearer branch to catch the express,". . .

Taunton station, on the Bristol to Exeter line, was opened in 1842, after which date passengers could travel to London by way of Bristol and Swindon. The shorter route from Taunton via Castle Cary was not constructed until 1905–06.

The Royal Horse Artillery arrive at Toneborough Barracks, Captain William de Stancy being among them.

The Jellalabad Barracks, in Mount Street, Taunton, was the depot of the Somerset Light Infantry, and the brick keep built in 1878–80 still remains.

Paula and Charlotte attend the hunt ball at Toneborough Town Hall.

The old Market House, in the centre of Taunton, was built in 1770–72, and comprised the Guildhall with open arcading on either side for market traders. The arcades have since been enclosed.

A 15th century canopied table-tomb monument in Dunster church, Somerset, commemorating a member of the Luttrell family, owners of Dunster Castle from 1376 until 1976. Lieutenant-Colonel Geoffrey Luttrell then gave it to the National Trust.

A Laodicean

The down-side entrance to the Whiteball railway tunnel at Werescote, near Wellington, Somerset. 39

12.   What the Shepherd Saw

THIS SHORT story is set in mid-Wessex, on Marlbury Downs (Marlborough Downs) where a young shepherd-boy concealed in his hut sees a midnight meeting between the Duchess Harriet and her cousin Captain Ogbourne (there are three Ogbourne villages north of Marlborough). The meeting takes place beside a prehistoric trilithon, and is misconstrued as a lovers' assignation by the Duke, who is also concealed nearby, with tragic consequences.

A renowned flock of sheep is kept on Marlbury Downs, and the shepherd's hut is placed at a spot known as Lambing Corner.

The Marlborough Downs, lie north-west of Marlborough, Wiltshire, and sheep are still to be found there.

Near the shepherd's hut "was a Druidical trilithon, consisting of three oblong stones in the form of a doorway, two on end and one across as a lintel. . . . The ruin was locally called the Devil's Door."

The Devil's Den, probably the remains of a Neolithic chambered long barrow, is situated on the downs about two miles west of Marlborough. It stands in Clatford Bottom.

The Duke and Duchess live at nearby Shakeforest Towers "where the great western road crossed before you came to the old park entrance". . . The house is "surmounted by parapets with square-cut battlements".

Clatford House lies just south of the A4 between Marlborough and Avebury, opposite the track leading to The Devil's Den. It fits Hardy's description geographically, if not architecturally.

The Devil's Den in Clatford Bottom on the Marlborough Downs, Wiltshire.

What the Shepherd Saw

13. Two on a Tower

AS STATED in his preface to the 1895 edition, Hardy's aim here was to set a small scale earthly romance against a back-cloth of astronomical scale. At the time of writing in 1882, Hardy was living in Wimborne, and Welland House with its associated tower and park is undoubtedly based on Charborough, particularly as the railway station at Warborne (Wimborne) which features several times in the novel is described as being five miles distant. To quote from the preface – "The scene of the action was suggested by two real spots in the part of the country specified, each of which has a column standing upon it. Certain surrounding peculiarities have been imported into the narrative from both sites, and from elsewhere." The chief imported item is the tree clad earthwork called Rings-Hill on which the tower stands, and this is generally considered to be based on Weatherby Castle near Milborne St Andrew, as stated by Lea. Another is the church near Welland House which is described as having a west tower and "semi Norman arches"; the small church at Charborough has neither, but the nearby church of Almer, which still retains close ties with Charborough, has a west tower and a Norman north arcade.

In the opening scene, Lady Constantine returns to her home at Welland Park in "a gleaming landau,"...

Charborough Park, beside the A31 five miles west of Wimborne, with its well-known brick boundary walls built in association with the re-alignment of the turnpike road in 1841–42.

Lady Viviette Constantine of Welland House begins to take an interest in the work of Swithin St Cleeve, a young astronomer who is allowed to use the nearby tower as an observatory.

Charborough House dates from the 17th century, with 18th and 19th century modifications. The tower was built in 1790 and rebuilt 40 feet higher after being struck by lightning in 1838.

The tower stands on a tree-clad ancient earthwork in the park, known as Rings-Hill.

Weatherby Castle is an Iron Age hill-fort near Milborne St Andrew. On the top is a brick obelisk erected in 1761.

The tower, known as Rings-Hill Speer is generally referred to as a column. It "had been erected in the eighteenth century,"... *and "had been built in the Tuscan order of classical architecture,".*..

Charborough Tower, being of early Gothic revival style and octagonal does not fit this description, but the Hood Monument at Butleigh in Somerset is in the form of a Tuscan column.

Swithin St Cleeve had been educated at Warborne Grammar School, "where they draw up young gam'sters' brains like rhubarb under a ninepenny pan,"...

The Queen Elizabeth Grammar School at Wimborne was founded in 1563, and the original school was totally rebuilt in 1849–50. It is now part of a residential development.

The parish church near Welland House has "semi-Norman arches", and at one point in the story Swithin "ascended to the belfry in the west tower,"... *in order to see into the adjoining garden.*

The parish church of St Mary at Almer contains an interesting and harmonious mixture of architectural styles, including a Norman arcade, a 15th century west tower and an 18th century nave.

Whilst staying in Bath, Viviette visits the abbey church where she spends some time in "wandering about beneath the aisles". . .

Bath abbey church, on the site of an earlier Norman church was begun in 1499. The interior is noted for its beautiful fan-vaulting.

On their journeys to Bath, Swithin and Viviette leave from Warborne station which lies five miles from Welland House.

Wimborne station, opened in 1847, originally lay on the Southampton to Dorchester line. After the opening of a line from West Moors to Salisbury in 1866, the route from Wimborne to Bath would have been by way of Salisbury.

Viviette is waiting on the platform of Bath station when Swithin arrives for their marriage in that city.

The first Bath station on the Great Western line was opened in 1841. After the opening of a line from Evercreech to Bath in 1874, the Somerset and Dorset line would have provided a more direct route from Wimborne.

Viviette's brother, Louis Glanville, visits the Bishop of Melchester at the "episcopal palace".

The Bishop's Palace in the cathedral close at Salisbury continued to be the bishop's residence until 1946. It is now the Cathedral School.

An engraving of Charborough House by J.H. Le Keux from Hutchins 3rd edition, volume 3 (1868).

The former Queen Elizabeth Grammar School at Wimborne.

14. A Tradition of 1804

THIS SHORT story, one of the Wessex Tales, is based upon a supposed legend that Napoleon himself landed secretly on the Dorset coast in an attempt to determine a suitable spot for his intended invasion.

Shepherd-boy Solomon Selby and his Uncle Job are watching over a flock of sheep on the downs above the Cove on a calm moonlit night.

They see two strange men, who have landed from a small boat on the shore below, looking at the coastline. To their surprise and consternation, Uncle Job recognises one of them as "Bonaparty, . . . the Corsican ogre".

Lulworth Cove features as 'Lulwind Cove' in other works, e.g. *Desperate Remedies* and *Far from the Madding Crowd.*

Napoleon Bonaparte (1769–1821), a Corsican by birth, rapidly rose through the ranks of the French army becoming a military dictator in 1799. He was Emperor of France 1804–14, and in 1815 was defeated at the Battle of Waterloo.

Lulworth Cove, with the spectacular uplifted strata of Stair Hole in the foreground. St. Aldhelm's Head can be seen in the distance on the horizon.

15.   The Three Strangers

IT WAS "the night of March 28, 182–," and during a christening party given by shepherd Fennel and his wife, three mysterious strangers arrive in succession at their lonely house known as Higher Crowstairs. It is situated on the downs near a right-angled junction of two footpaths "not three miles" from the county town of Casterbridge (Dorchester). Lea suggests that Higher Crowstairs is in the vicinity of Grimstone Down, but this is more than four miles from Dorchester, and as the third stranger is travelling on foot from Shottsford (Blandford) to visit his condemned brother in Casterbridge jail, it is not conceivable that his path should have lain so far to the west. A spot on Waterston Ridge, just under three miles from Dorchester, seems more likely, when the route of the stranger from Blandford could have been on byways and footpaths by way of Milton Abbas, Cheselbourne, Muston, Waterston Ridge and Frome Whitfield, leading straight to Dorchester prison.

Higher Crowstairs is an isolated cottage on the downs "not three miles from a county-town", standing near "the crossing of two footpaths at right angles,". . .

On Waterston Ridge, just under three miles north of Dorchester there is a junction of two old trackways. An isolated modern farm building now stands there.

The first stranger is a condemned prisoner who has just escaped from Casterbridge jail, and the second is the hangman on his way there to execute him.

Dorchester prison was first built on its present site in 1790–92, and the original central archway was retained when the prison was totally rebuilt in 1884–85.

The third stranger has travelled from Shottsford, and was on his way to visit his condemned brother in Casterbridge jail.

Blandford Forum is a fine Georgian town, almost totally rebuilt after the disastrous fire of 1731.

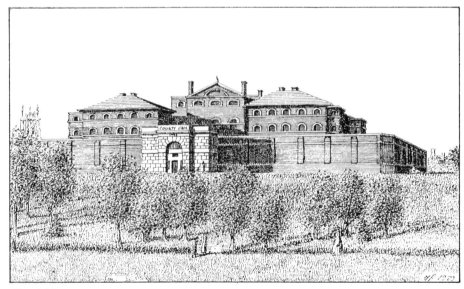

The old County Prison at Dorchester. Drawing based on a watercolour of 1796 by W. Upham.

16. The Romantic Adventures of a Milkmaid

'A WESSEX Cinderella' might have been an appropriate sub-title for this novelette which features milkmaid Margery Tucker in the title role, with Baron von Xanten as a combined Fairy Godfather and Prince Charming. The setting is the Exe valley north of Exonbury (Exeter) in the 1840s.

Margery Tucker, a milkmaid, lives and works with her father at Silverthorne Dairy-house in the valley of the Exe.

Up Exe Farm is situated between Silverton and Thorverton in the Exe valley about five miles north of Exeter.

Returning from her grandmother's cottage, Margery takes a short cut through the grounds of Mount Lodge, "a picturesque old country-house, . . . It was a building of the medium size, and unpretending, the facade being of stone;". . .

Killerton House, two and a half miles south east of Up Exe, was built in 1778–79, the architect being John Johnson. It was considerably extended to the north in the 19th century, and has belonged to the National Trust since 1944.

Believing the house to be unoccupied, Margery is surprised to find a foreign-looking gentleman sitting in the summer-house.

'The Bear's Hut' is an early 19th century timber and thatch summerhouse in the grounds of Killerton House.

Margery meets Baron von Xanten in Chillington Wood, where she changes into her ball-gown inside a large hollow tree.

Some very ancient trees still remain on the wooded slopes adjoining Killerton House.

The Baron takes Margery to a fashionable ball at the house of Lord Toneborough "in the next county".

The reference to Lord Toneborough indicates the Taunton area, possibly Hatch Beauchamp.

Jim Hayward, Margery's fiancé; is a lime-burner with a kiln in the hills bordering the valley near an ancient earthwork.

Dolbury is an earthwork at Killerton Clump on the top of the hill north of Killerton House. Nearby is a disused quarry.

A travelling musician asks Jim Hayward the shortest way to Tivworthy.

Tiverton is an old Devonshire town, 12 miles up the Exe valley from Exeter.

Margery goes to the Yeomanry Review at Exonbury where Jim Hayward is on parade in his resplendent scarlet uniform.

Exeter is an ancient city where the beautiful cathedral is almost entirely of the 14th century.

Margery accompanies Baron von Xanten to Idmouth, where his yacht is anchored off the coast.

Sidmouth is a south Devon seaside resort about 12 miles east of Exeter.

17.   Interlopers at the Knap

THE FICTIONAL Hintock villages which figure so prominently in *The Woodlanders* are first referred to in this short story, one of the Wessex Tales, and King's-Hintock, being described as lying "only a mile or two from King's-Hintock Court", (Melbury House) must refer to Melbury Osmond. Long Ash Lane, now the busy A37 Dorchester-Yeovil road, was during the 19th century a deserted track over the downs for much of its length with no villages to break the monotony or to provide rest and refreshment for travellers and their horses. Its decline began after the Maiden Newton Turnpike Trust had been set up in 1778 and lasted until the 1930s when the increase in motor traffic caused the old more direct route to again be favoured.

On a dark winter's evening, farmer Charles Darton and his companion Japheth Johns are travelling on horseback along lonely Long-Ash Lane from Casterbridge towards King's-Hintock.

The A37 Dorchester-Yeovil road follows the Roman road from Durnovaria (Dorchester) to Lindinis (Ilchester) for most of its length, and was itself constructed on the route of an even earlier trackway.

Their destination is "an old house with mullioned windows of Ham-hill stone," . . . at King's-Hintock where Sally Hall and her mother live.

Melbury Osmond is a delightful secluded village of mellow stone and thatch.

Sally Hall's brother Philip says "we passed through Evershead . . . and I just looked in at the Sow-and-Acorn". . . .

The Acorn Inn, Evershot.

Japheth Johns "withdrew for the night, going off to the roadside inn half-a-mile ahead," . . .

The Rest and Welcome Inn lies on the main A37 road near Melbury Osmond.

When Helena Hall's son goes to live with Charles Darton, he is handed over at. . . "'the White Horse', the fine old Elizabethan inn at Chalk Newton". . .

The White Horse at Maiden Newton, now closed (1989), was built about 1900 on the site of its predecessor which was a fine old thatched Elizabethan coaching inn.

The White Horse Inn at Maiden Newton. Drawing of the former building based on a watercolour by E.S. Beach and old photographs.

18. A Mere Interlude

'SOUTH WESSEX', approximating to Hardy's native county of Dorset, is the setting for most of his novels and short stories, but Cornwall, as suggested by the term 'Off-Wessex', seems to have been regarded as outside the confines of the fictional 'Wessex' proper. Nevertheless, that county is the scene of two works, most notably the novel *A Pair of Blue Eyes*, and this short story which is centred on Pen-zephyr (Penzance) and the Isles of Lyonesse (The Isles of Scilly). No particular date for the story is mentioned, but it is presumably set in the late 1870s, as the 'pro-cathedral' at Trufal (Truro) is referred to. Cornwall became a new diocese in 1876 with Truro as its See, when the parish church of St Mary served as a temporary cathedral (i.e. a pro-cathedral) until 1880 when work began on the new cathedral on the same site.

Baptista Trewthen, a young mistress at a country school near Tor-upon-Sea, is about to return home to the Isles of Lyonesse where she is to be married to an old friend of the family.

Torquay, the well known south Devon seaside resort, has grown considerably in the last 100 years or so.

Being delayed at Pen-zephyr, Baptista visits the pier and harbour and meets a former lover, Charles Stow.

Penzance, the most westerly town in Cornwall (and England), is the port of departure for sea crossings to the Isles of Scilly.

Baptista agrees to marry Charles on the spur of the moment, and they take a train from Pen-zephyr station up the line to Trufal.

The line from Penzance to Truro was opened in 1852, Truro station being a terminus until 1859 when the connection with Plymouth was made.

In Trufal they take up lodgings in different parts of the city whilst waiting for their marriage licence. "On Sunday she saw him . . . across the nave of the pro-cathedral."

The parish church of Truro served as a pro-cathedral from 1876, when the new diocese was formed, until 1880, when it was demolished to make way for the new cathedral.

On the way back to Pen-zephyr after their early morning marriage, Charles takes a swim near St Michael's Mount, and is drowned.

St Michael's Mount, Marazion, an island at high tide, was a priory belonging to Mont S. Michel in France from the 11th century until 1425. It gives its name to Mount's Bay.

Having become a widow only hours after her hasty marriage, Baptista takes the steamer home to the Isles of Lyonesse, passing by Mousehole and St Clements Isle.

St Clements Isle lies just offshore near Mousehole, which is a picturesque Cornish fishing village south of Penzance.

On arrival at St Maria's, Baptista is met by her parents at "the pier of Giant's Town". . .

Hugh Town is the principal town and landing place on the largest of the Scilly islands, St Mary's.

David Heddegan goes to the church to check the arrangements for his marriage to Baptista.

The church in Hugh Town, known as 'New Church' is a relatively plain building of 1835.

Whilst on honeymoon at Pen-zephyr, Baptista slips away for a few hours, and goes by rail to Redrutin where she attends the funeral of Charles Stow.

Redruth, a Cornish town, now somewhat industrialised, lies between Penzance and Truro. The railway line from Penzance was opened in 1852.

The old parish church of Truro, Cornwall, which was almost totally demolished in 1880 to make way for the new cathedral on the same site. An engraving of 1802 by J. Britton and J. Smith from The Beauties of England and Wales, volume 2 (1807).

St. Michael's Mount, off Marazion, Cornwall. An engraving by William George Maton from his Observations relative to the Western Counties of England, published in 1797.

A Mere Interlude

19. A Tryst at an Ancient Earthwork

ON A dark and stormy night an archaeologist and his friend meet at an ancient earthwork and carry out a clandestine and hasty excavation in order to test a theory that the hill-fort had been occupied in Roman times. Although not named, the earthwork is generally assumed to be Maiden Castle near Dorchester, and the story (written in 1885) was probably prompted by Edward Cunnington's excavation of a Roman building there in 1882–84.

The archaeologist and his friend meet on the earthwork under cover of darkness, and the excavation is begun by the light of a lantern.

Maiden Castle, the largest and most spectacular hill-fort in England, originated during the Neolithic period, and was enlarged and developed in four separate phases during the Iron Age. It was later captured and occupied by the Romans.

Work is commenced at "an elevation in the sod, a suggested squareness amid a mass of irregularities around," and at about a foot depth a mosaic pavement is found.

The foundations of a Roman building on Maiden Castle were first excavated in 1882–84 and were later identified as a temple by Wheeler in his excavations of 1934–38.

Several small finds are unearthed, but the most significant is "a small image four or five inches high . . . a figure of Mercury,". . .

A 4½ inch high "brass image of a Roman deity" was dug up in the back garden of the 'free school' in Dorchester in 1747, and was illustrated in all three editions of Hutchins.

All the objects found that night were meticulously replaced, or so the narrator was led to believe, but after the archaeologist's death "a gilt statuette representing Mercury" was found among his possessions and "bequeathed to the Casterbridge Museum".

The County Museum at Dorchester was built on its present site in 1881, the architect being George Crickmay of Weymouth. The figure of Mercury referred to may still be found in the Roman gallery of the museum.

The foundations of a Roman temple inside Maiden Castle, near Dorchester.

The figure of Mercury illustrated in all three editions of Hutchins.

20. The Mayor of Casterbridge

BEING THE county town of South Wessex, Casterbridge (Dorchester) is referred to in most of the Wessex novels and short stories, but here it comes to the fore as the setting for almost the whole of this great and well-known novel. The story begins as a kind of prologue at Weydon-Priors in Upper Wessex "before the nineteenth century had reached one-third of its span," but the main part takes place in Casterbridge some 18–20 years later, a more precise date being suggested by the statement that "The railway had stretched out an arm towards Casterbridge . . . but had not reached it by several miles as yet." The Southampton to Dorchester line was opened on 1 June 1847.

Until the 1840s Dorchester was still largely confined within the limits of its old Roman walls, marked by tree-lined walks, with Fordington as a separate village lying immediately to the east with a tenuous link at the bottom of High East Street. Since then the town has expanded to the south and west, but the general character of the main High East and High West Streets remains remarkably unchanged even though several individual buildings have been rebuilt. South Street, now the principal shopping street, has changed more, being formerly largely residential, with the wider Cornhill end and its junction with the two High Streets forming the market-place.

All the following references are to Dorchester unless otherwise stated:

Whilst in a drunken state, the young Michael Henchard rashly sells his wife Susan at Weydon-Priors Fair.

Weyhill in Hampshire lies on the A303, three miles west of Andover. The ancient fair continued until the Second World War. In 1990 the derelict cob and slate fair booths still stood by the roadside near the church.

Some 18 years later Susan Henchard/ Newson and her daughter Elizabeth-Jane are approaching Casterbridge and pause to look at the town from Mellstock Hill.

The view of Dorchester from Stinsford Hill is still one of the best, as the old part of the town can be seen rather than the suburban areas to the south and west.

"The travellers returned into the High Street, where there were timber houses with overhanging stories,". . .

6 and 7 High West Street are early 17th century timber framed houses. Number 6 is best known for having been Judge Jeffreys' lodging during The Bloody Assizes of 1685.

The King's Arms was "the chief hotel in Casterbridge. . . A spacious bow-window projected into the street over the main portico," . . . and here Mayor Henchard presided over the corporation dinner.

The King's Arms Hotel is a fine old coaching inn with an impressive entrance portico and bow window.

Donald Farfrae is staying at a smaller inn further down the street – The Three Mariners.

The old Three Mariners, an Elizabethan building, was replaced by the present one later in the 19th century.

Mayor Henchard's house is situated in Corn Street, and "was one of the best, faced with dull red-and-grey old brick".	10 South Street, a fine 18th century town house, is now Barclay's Bank.
Henchard accompanies Farfrae along Chalk Walk as far as the corner where a "footpath ran steeply down the slope"...	Colliton Walk, where a steep footpath still runs down the bank to the Grove at the north west corner of the old walls.
Henchard and Susan meet again after 18 years or so at The Ring, a Roman Ampitheatre just outside the town.	Maumbury Rings, originally a Neolithic henge monument, was converted into an amphitheatre in Roman times.
Susan and Elizabeth-Jane occupy a cottage "in the upper or western part of the town, near the Roman wall,"...	A small section of Roman stonework which formed part of the west wall still remains between Top o' Town and Princes Street.
After a respectable interval Michael Henchard and 'widow Newson' re-marry at the church.	The parish church for the west end of the town was Holy Trinity. The mediaeval church had been rebuilt in 1824 (It was again rebuilt in 1875).
Adjoining Casterbridge on the east is Durnover. "Here wheat-ricks overhung the old Roman street, and thrust their eaves against the church tower;"...	St George's church, Fordington, was considerably lengthened in phases between 1907 and 1928, thus destroying the Georgian chancel of 1750. The tower survives but not the adjoining farmyard.
"Close to the town was an elevated green spot surrounded by an ancient square earthwork".... Here Mayor Henchard's fête was washed out by rain.	Poundbury is an Iron Age hill-fort lying just to the north west of Dorchester.
Farfrae's successful fête was held in the West Walk under rick cloths "hung up to the arching trees,"...	West Walks is one of a series of tree-lined walks following the route of the old Roman walls.
After the fête Farfrae escorts Elizabeth-Jane home, and they pass along Bowling Walk.	Bowling Alley Walk follows part of the southern boundary of the Roman town.
Lucetta Templeman intends to pass through Casterbridge – "I shall be in the coach which changes horses at the Antelope Hotel"...	The Antelope Hotel in Cornhill is a fine old coaching inn with some portions dating from c1600. It closed as a hotel on 18 March 1989.
"At the town-pump there were gathered ... a few old inhabitants, who came there for water".... It was also a favourite spot for exchanging local gossip.	The old town pump in Cornhill was erected in 1784 on the site of an old market house which was in the form of a cupola.
Returning home Henchard "went on past the cottage in which the old local hangman had lived"...	Hangman's Cottage stands by the riverside, on the north side of the town.
Lucetta comes to live in Casterbridge and takes up residence in High-Place Hall.	Colliton House. Its former grounds now form the County Hall site. Hardy places it some distance to the south east of its true position.

At the back of High-Place Hall there was an archway – "the keystone of the arch was a mask" . . . which had been damaged by boys throwing stones at it.	The archway which formerly led to a yard and brewhouse at the rear of Colliton House is preserved in the County Museum above the library door.
Lucetta suggests that Elizabeth-Jane should visit the local museum – "It is an old house in a back street". . .	3 Trinity Street, a fine 18th century town house, was the County Museum after 1851. Trinity Street was then known as South Back Street.
After their estrangement Henchard and Farfrae meet by chance "in the chestnut-walk which ran along the south wall of the town".	South Walks follow the course of the Roman wall from The Junction at the end of South Street to Icen Way.
"The . . . Market House and Town Hall abutted against . . . the Church except in the lower storey, where an arched thoroughfare gave admittance to a large square called Bull Stake."	The old town hall had a relatively short life, being built in 1792 and replaced by the present building in 1848. A narrow roadway now leads to North Square.
Lucetta and Elizabeth-Jane are rescued from a bull by Henchard at a barn near the end of the avenue on the Port-Bredy road.	A former barn known as Damer's Barn on the Bridport Road no longer exists.
After his bankruptcy, Henchard goes to live at "Jopp's cottage by the Priory Mill". . .	The Friary Mill was situated by the river on the north side of the town at the bottom of Friary Hill.
"Two bridges stood near the lower part of Casterbridge town. The first, of weather-stained brick, was immediately at the end of High Street, . . . The second bridge, of stone, was further out". . .	The former brick Swan Bridge at the bottom of High East Street was replaced by a stone one in 1954. The stone Grey's Bridge of 1748 still remains.
Mixen Lane in Durnover was a squalid area of slum dwellings where the only things that flourished were vice and crime.	Mill Lane, Fordington. Most of the old cottages had been pulled down by the time the novel was written in 1884–85.
Henchard tries to intercept Farfrae where the Mellstock Road branches off from the road from Weatherbury.	Cuckoo Corner is the point where Cuckoo Lane, leading to Bockhampton, branches off the A35. This junction was considerably altered in 1991–92.
Henchard contemplates suicide at Ten Hatches Weir.	Ten Hatches Weir survives, a little way upstream from Grey's Bridge. Only five hatches now remain complete.
Henchard takes on a small seed and grain shop "overlooking the churchyard".	63 High West Street. Before the 1875 rebuilding, Holy Trinity churchyard extended to the street frontage.
Henchard often went to "the prehistoric fort called Mai Dun, of huge dimensions and many ramparts,". . .	Maiden Castle. (See *A Tryst at an Ancient Earthwork*)
In Shottsford, Henchard buys some new clothes and a wedding present for Elizabeth-Jane.	Blandford Forum is a fine 18th century town rebuilt after the great fire of 1731.

Henchard's last days are spent in a derelict cottage near "the heath to the north of Anglebury," near "a blasted clump of firs on the summit of a hill,". . .

Lea indicates that this refers to Beacon Hill, a prominent landmark on the heath between Corfe Mullen and Upton.

The old Three Mariners Inn, High East Street, Dorchester. Elevational drawing based on a sketch by Thomas Hardy.

Below, the former Friary Mill, Dorchester. Drawing based on old photographs and a watercolour of 1884 by Henry Moule. Later, the mill building itself was demolished, leaving the waterwheel exposed.

The Mayor of Casterbridge

21. The Waiting Supper

STAFFORD HOUSE, featuring as Froom-Everard House, is the setting for this short story which concerns a frustrated romance between the squire's daughter and a young local yeoman farmer. During the Middle Ages this part of West Stafford was a separate parish known as Frome Belet, and previous owners of the manor included the Longs and the Everards, both names being used for the principal characters, Nicholas Long and Christine Everard. The story begins in 1837 ('50 years ago' when written in 1887) and after a lapse of 15 years, resumes in 1852, concluding c1870.

Froom-Everard House is the home of Squire Everard and his daughter Christine.

Stafford House is a fine building of 1633 incorporating part of an earlier house. It was extended in 1848–50.

Nicholas Long's farm is at Elsenford across the meadows in "the adjoining parish".

Duddle Farm is on the opposite side of the Frome valley, just within Puddletown parish.

Nicholas and Christine go to her parish church to be secretly married, but the rector refuses.

West Stafford Church was rebuilt in 1640 with the exception of the 16th century tower. The chancel was added in 1898–99.

Christine and her father attend a Christening party at Athelhall where dancing is held on the lawn.

Athelhampton Hall is a beautiful house of mainly 15th and 16th century date. A former gatehouse was demolished in 1862.

The hall is "covered with a fine open-timbered roof, whose braces purlins and rafters made a brown thicket of oak overhead".

The interior of the hall at Athelhampton is noted for its fine open timbered roof and oriel window.

Nicholas and Christine meet in 'The Sallows', a riverside plantation near Froom-Everard House where there is a waterfall.

A waterfall still remains on a branch of the Frome in a wooded area to the north of Stafford House.

Christine goes shopping in the High Street of the nearby market town.

High West or High East Street, Dorchester.

Nicholas "stood on the hill above Shottsford-Forum, and awaited a coach" to Melchester and London.

Blandford Forum, probably Dorchester Hill.

After an absence of 15 years, Nicholas returns to the neighbourhood and stays at the Buck's Head Inn at Roy-Town.

Troytown near Puddletown. The inn also features in *Far from the Madding Crowd*.

Nicholas walks on the heath towards Froom-Everard and can discern "a clump of trees standing on a barrow".

Rainbarrows are in a direct line across the heath between Troytown and West Stafford.

Nicholas and Christine meet again "on the open down by a pond,". . .

Rushy Pond on Black Heath, Stinsford.

James Bellston, Christine's long-lost husband who was presumed dead, is said to have arrived at Casterbridge station.

Nicholas has a cottage built on the other side of the river, near Froom-Everard House.

Dorchester (South) station, then the terminus of the Southampton-Dorchester railway, was opened on 1 June 1847.

Keeper's Cottage stands in the meadows to the north west of Stafford House.

Stafford House, West Stafford, near Dorchester. An engraving by J.H. Le Keux from Hutchins 3rd edition, volume 2 (1863).

Athelhampton Hall, near Puddletown. A photolithograph from John Pouncy's Dorsetshire Photographically Illustrated (1857).

22.   Alicias's Diary

AS THE title implies, this short story takes the form of entries in the diary of a young lady, the daughter of the rector of Wherryborne. There are few clues as to the whereabouts of the rectory, but from various references it is evidently not too far from Budmouth-Regis (Weymouth), and a letter posted there at daybreak reached Wherryborne Rectory the same afternoon. As Hardy began living at Max Gate in 1885, two years before this story was written, it is possible that he may have had the nearby Winterborne Came Rectory in mind, particularly as there is a slight similarity in name.

Wherryborne Rectory is the home of Alicia, her sister and parents, her father being the rector.

The Old Rectory at Winterborne Came is best known for having been the home of William Barnes from 1862 until his death in 1886.

Alicia, Caroline and Charles de la Feste go walking in Wherryborne Wood.

North Plantation on Conygar Hill lies just to the south of Winterborne Came Old Rectory.

Caroline and Charles are married in the parish church at Wherryborne.

The parish church of St Peter at Winterborne Came was built in the 14th century and extended in the 15th.

The beautiful old rectory of Winterborne Came. It stands beside the A352 road to Wareham less than a mile south-east of Dorchester, and within sight of Max Gate, Hardy's own house which was completed in 1885. Hardy visited William Barnes at the rectory on 22 July 1883.   *Alicias's Diary*

23. The Woodlanders

HERE, AS in *The Return of the Native*, Hardy's masterful descriptions of Wessex scenery come to the fore as an appropriate backdrop against which the characters portrayed come to life, yet at the same time seem as much a part of the woodland scene as the trees themselves. Again, as in the case of the heathland of the earlier novel, the densely wooded area described has undergone considerable changes, giving rise to much speculation as to the exact whereabouts of the Hintock villages which figure so prominently. From an earlier short story, *Interlopers at the Knap*, there can be little doubt that King's Hintock refers to Melbury Osmond, and the choice of Melbury as a surname for two of the principal characters in *The Woodlanders*, suggests that the Hintocks were originally intended to be more closely equated with the Melbury villages. However, as certain aspects of the novel were likely to be considered immoral in Victorian eyes, Hardy, in an attempt to avoid any possible allusions to real people, seems deliberately to have made some of the locations difficult to identify precisely – even some of the fictional characters encountered difficulties in finding Little Hintock.

The territory in which *The Woodlanders* is set can perhaps best be considered as a composite area comprising the neighbourhood of Bubb Down Hill in the west, where Melbury Bubb and Stockwood could represent Great and Little Hintock respectively, extending eastwards to High Stoy Hill and Dogbury Hill, where their counterparts could be Minterne Magna and Hermitage.

Whatever uncertainties there may be in the locations, the date of the story is firmly established by several references. The new divorce laws are said to have been enacted "twenty and twenty-one Vic.", (i.e. 1857–58), and at the end of the story the Earl of Wessex Hotel at Sherton Abbas is said to have been recently rebuilt "contemporaneously with the construction of the railway", the line through Sherborne having been opened in 1860. Also near the end of the novel, Barber Percomb, who features in the opening scene, states that he last visited Little Hintock "some three year ago", so that the period 1857–60 is clearly indicated.

Little Hintock is a small village in the woodland, and "the commanding heights called High-Stoy and Bubb-Down Hill overlook the landscape in which it is supposed to be hid".	Probably an amalgamation of Stockwood and Hermitage. At Stockwood there is a tiny church dedicated to St Edwold.
Giles Winterborne regularly attends the market at Sherton Abbas.	The former market place at Sherborne is at the junction of Cheap Street and Long Street.
On their way out of the town Giles and Grace drive past "Sherton Abbas Park and Castle".	Sherborne Lodge (or 'new castle') was built for Sir Walter Raleigh in the 1590s. It was enlarged in 1625.
Mrs Charmond lives at Hintock House – "it stood in a hole," . . . and "its walls were surmounted by a battlemented parapet;". . .	Turnworth House was built about 1800 and has now been demolished. (Hardy was concerned in the restoration of Turnworth church in 1869).

Dr Fitzpiers is said to be descended from an ancient family whose name is perpetuated in the village of Oakbury-Fitzpiers.	Okeford Fitzpaine is one of the three Okeford villages.
George Melbury passes through the churchyard at Little Hintock on his way home.	Probably the church of St Edwold at Stockwood or St Mary at Hermitage.
The woodmen discuss local traditions including one associated with King's Hintock Court "a few miles off". . .	Melbury House. (It features more fully in A Group of Noble Dames.)
At a gathering on old midsummer eve, some of the girls are from Great Hintock.	Probably an amalgamation of Melbury Bubb and Minterne Magna.
Grace Melbury visits the ruins of Sherton Castle.	The old Norman castle at Sherborne was largely destroyed during the Civil Wars.
"The chief hotel at Sherton Abbas was the 'Earl of Wessex' – a substantial inn of Ham-hill stone". . .	The former Digby Hotel in Digby Road was rebuilt c1860 and now forms part of Sherborne Boys' School.
Mrs Charmond goes to stay with friends at Middleton Abbey for a while.	Milton Abbey House (now a school) was built in 1771–76, the architect being Sir William Chambers.
Dr Fitzpiers leans on a gate "on High-Stoy Hill, some way from Little Hintock,". . .	High Stoy Hill lies just to the north west of Minterne Magna.
Dr Fitzpiers and Grace "ascended towards the base of High-Stoy and Dogbury Hill,". . .	Eastwards from High Stoy Hill is the distinctive outline of Dogbury Hill.
Giles Winterborne sees Dr Fitzpiers "near Reveller's Inn", which is the scene later of a visit by the Tim Tangs wedding party.	Lower Revels farm lies south of Middlemarsh. It occurs as 'Revels Inn' in trade directories up to 1855, but as 'Revels Farm' after that date.
Whilst Dr Fitzpiers' horse is drinking at Lydden Spring, he hears the clock of Newland Buckton strike twelve.	The little River Lydden rises at Buckland Newton and flows northwards towards Lydlinch.
Grace visits a friend at Shottsford-Forum.	Blandford Forum.
George Melbury meets a dubious lawyer by the conduit at Sherton Abbas.	The conduit at Sherborne is a 16th century wash-house formerly in the abbey precincts.
When in Sherton Abbas, Grace meets Giles in Sheep Street.	Cheap Street is the principal shopping street of Sherborne.
They go into the abbey church at Sherton Abbas.	The interior of Sherborne abbey church is notable for its beautiful 15th century fan vaulting.
Giles Winterborne spends his last days in "One-chimney Hut, by Delborough," . . .	Probably in the woodlands to the northwest of Melbury House near Lewcombe in East Chelborough parish.

Tim Tangs' wedding party parades around the district, including Reveller's Inn and Marshwood.

Lower Revels Farm, already referred to, and Middlemarsh.

The former Turnworth House, between Winterborne Stickland and Okeford Fitzpaine. An engraving by Philip Brannon from Hutchins 3rd edition volume 3 (1868). Hardy's description of 'Hintock House' – 'It stood in a hole' – could well have been a description of this engraving.

The magnificent vaulted interior of Sherborne Abbey church. An engraving by Philip Brannon from Hutchins 3rd edition, volume 4 (1873).

24. The Withered Arm

THIS RATHER gruesome tale is set in an area bordering the Frome valley and the heath, at Holmstoke, which as the name implies, is based on an amalgamation of West and East Holme and East Stoke. East Stoke proper is situated on the south side of the river where the overgrown ruins of the old parish church still remain in a circular churchyard in the meadows. The story takes place during 1819–25 as indicated by Conjurer Trendle's remark, which occurs six years after the beginning of the tale – "The last I sent was in '13 – near twelve years ago."

Farmer Lodge is travelling from Anglebury to Holmstoke, bringing home his young bride.

Their route from Wareham would probably have been by way of Holme Lane.

Farmer Lodge's house is "a white house of ample dimensions".

The 17th century West Holme Manor was formerly a farmhouse.

Rhoda Brook lives in a lonely cottage in a lane near the heath a mile and a half on the Anglebury side of farmer Lodge's house.

Probably the small lane off Holme Lane in the neighbourhood of East Holme Farm.

Rhoda sends her son to the Sunday morning service at Holmstoke church, so that he can report on the appearance of the new Mrs Lodge.

The ruin of the old East Stoke church still stands in the meadows. It was abandoned in 1828 when the new church was built by the main road.

Rhoda's son goes to the church, and when he "reached the ancient little pile" . . . took his seat by the font.

The 13th century font from the old church still remains, having been re-used in the 1828 church.

Gertrude Lodge, on horseback, nears the edge of the heath towards Casterbridge. Here she "halted before a pool called Rushy Pond,". . .

Rushy Pond lies near the edge of the heath a little to the south east of Hardy's cottage.

Gertrude arrives in Casterbridge and stays at the White Hart.

The White Hart at the lower end of High East Street, Dorchester, has been rebuilt since the 19th century.

She visits the hangman at his cottage to seek his assistance in her gruesome task.

Hangman's Cottage stands on the north side of Dorchester by the riverside.

Gertrude secretly enters the prison shortly after the young man has been hanged.

The old county prison at Dorchester was built in 1790–92. It was later rebuilt in 1884–85.

The White Hart, Dorchester. Elevational drawing of the former building, compiled from various old photographs.

         The Withered Arm

25. A Tragedy of Two Ambitions

THE HALBOROUGH brothers are studying to become priests, but their ambitions are constantly in jeopardy on account of their lazy, uncouth and frequently drunken father. When their sister becomes engaged to the local landowner at Narrobourne, their father, alas, sets out to call on his future son-in-law. However, being drunk as usual, he falls into a weir and is drowned, before reaching the manor house – but could the brothers, who were nearby, have saved him if they had acted more promptly?

Joshua Halborough is studying at Fountall Theological College in the cathedral close.

Wells Theological College, founded in 1840 in part of Vicar's Close, was moved to the old Archdeaconry house in 1890.

Joshua sees his father "staring quizzically at the west front of the cathedral,". . .

Wells Cathedral, one of the most beautiful in England, is mostly of the 13th and 14th centuries.

Joshua takes up his first appointment as curate at the parish church of Narrobourne.

The parish church of St Martin, West Coker, was largely rebuilt in 1863–64.

Joshua is invited to Narrobourne manor house by Mr Fellmer.

The beautiful manor house of West Coker was rebuilt in 1457 after a fire.

Old Mr Halborough is serving a seven days prison sentence at Fountall gaol.

The old gaol at Wells still remains behind the town hall, but has been somewhat modified.

After his release, Mr Halborough asks his two sons to meet him at the Castle Inn, Ivell.

The former Castle Inn in Middle Street, Yeovil, was originally a mediaeval chantry. It was demolished in the 1920s.

The Halborough brothers recollect passing a man in the dark "on the other side of Hendford Hill,". . .

Hendford Hill was, and is, the main road exit south-westwards out of Yeovil. The A30 ascends it, from the modern police station, to the junction at the top where the Roman road, now the A37, goes south towards Dorchester. Rodney Legg writes that in Hardy's time, when he lived in Yeovil, this corner was cut by a deep-cut track which curves through the trees to the east and still exists as a public bridleway. From the junction the road to the west, the A30, continues along the top of the hill to the White Post and then descends into West Coker.

Old Mr Halborough is "rather the worse for liquor", and in taking a shorter route to Narrobourne in the darkness, falls into a weir and is drowned.

The former mill pond at Holywell near West Coker is now represented by a small stream running through a garden of the converted mill. Nearby is a small weir.

26.   The Melancholy Hussar of the German Legion

IN THE days of King George III (1760–1820), there was a German Legion of specialised troops within the British army, and these were usually in attendance during the king's annual visits to Weymouth between 1789 and 1805. During the summer of 1801 the Legion was in camp on the downs near Bincombe, and in the parish register for 30th June that year is recorded the burial of two German hussars, Matthäus Tina and Christoph Bless, both aged 22, who had been shot for desertion. That real event forms the basis for this short story, one of the Wessex Tales.

Phyllis Grove lives with her father in a "small, dilapidated, half farm, half manor-house", which "stood somewhat apart" at the upper end of the village. Phyllis and Matthäus regularly meet by the garden wall.

The quiet and secluded little village of Bincombe lies about a mile from the busy Dorchester to Weymouth road.

Matthäus plans to desert from the army and return to Germany, taking Phyllis with him. They are to be accompanied by Christoph, who is to procure a boat and "row it round the Nothe – or Look-out as it was called in those days". . . .

The Nothe at Weymouth has been the site of a gun emplacement since the 17th century, but the present Palmerstonian fort was constructed between 1860 and 1872.

The two deserters are caught and shot, their bodies being buried in unmarked graves in the local churchyard.

Bincombe church was first built c1200, and was to a large extent rebuilt in the 15th century.

Bincombe church. An engraving originally published in The Gentleman's Magazine, *and reproduced in* Hutchins 2nd edition, *volume 4 (1815).*

A trooper of the 3rd Hussars, the King's German Legion, about 1815.

27. A Group of Noble Dames

ON A wet day, members of the South-Wessex Field and Antiquarian Club abandon a proposed outdoor meeting, and instead remain in the museum where they relate traditional stories concerning ladies of local aristocratic families in bygone days. This provides the framework for a group of historical sketches having a common theme, most of the bare facts being gleaned from actual pedigrees published in Hutchins' *History of Dorset* which Hardy clothed in fiction based on tradition.

(a) *The First Countess of Wessex*. Here the setting is King's-Hintock Court, and the characters Susan and Thomas Dornell and their only child Betty who marries Stephen Reynard at the early age of 13, are readily identifiable from this extract from the Fox-Strangways pedigree in Hutchins 3rd edition:-

Thomas Horner   = Susanna Strangways
of Mells Park, Somerset | of Melbury Sampford
d.1741   b.1690 m.1713 d.1758

Stephen Fox   = Elizabeth Strangways Horner
b.1706 d.1776   b.1723 m.1736 d.1792
became Lord Ilchester 1741,
and Earl of Ilchester 1758

Mrs Susan Dornell, heiress of the family estates, her husband Thomas and their daughter Betty, live at King's-Hintock Court.	Melbury House is of 16th century origin with 17th century extensions. It was considerably enlarged in 1872 and 1884–85.
Thomas Dornell's family home is at Falls-Park where he still sometimes resides.	Mells Park, Somerset, belonged to the Horner family until relatively recent times. It was largely rebuilt in 1923.
Squire Dornell's servant "took a seat in the chimney-corner of the Sow-and-Acorn" at Evershead.	The Acorn Inn at Evershot.
Betty refers to "their own little church in the shrubbery of King's-Hintock Court".	The parish church of St Mary, Melbury Sampford, lies close to Melbury House. It was rebuilt c1440.
Young Charley Phelipson of Elm-Cranlynch would have been preferred as a husband for Betty by her father.	Court House, Corfe Mullen, is a small part of what was once a much larger Elizabethan House. It belonged to a branch of the Phelips family of Montacute until the 18th century.
After her husband's death Mrs Susan Dornell, "among other acts of pious devotion . . . rebuilt the church of King's-Hintock village,". . .	The parish church of Melbury Osmond was rebuilt in 1745 at the expense of Mrs Susanna Strangways-Horner of Melbury House.

Betty, now 18, has been meeting her husband, Stephen Reynard, secretly, including "Once at Abbot's-Cernel in the ruined chamber over the gatehouse."	The Abbot's Hall at Cerne Abbey was built c1500, but all that now remains is the porch which is often referred to as the gatehouse.

(b) *Barbara of the House of Grebe.* As in the previous story the fictional characters – Lord Uplandtowers of Knollingwood Hall, and Sir John and Lady Grebe and their daughter Barbara of Chene Manor – are readily identifiable from the pedigree of the Webb family of Canford Magna, as reproduced in Hutchins 3rd edition, of which the following is an extract:-

Sir John Webb of   = Mary, daughter of Thomas Salvaine of
Great Canford, Bart.   Easingwold, York
d.1797   d.1782

Anthony Ashley-Cooper   = Barbara, daughter and eventual sole
5th Earl of Shaftesbury   heiress
b.1761 d.1811   b.1762 m.1786 d.1819

The two family estates featuring in the story lie about ten miles apart, each adjoining the new turnpike road connecting Havenpool and Warborne with Melchester.	The turnpike road from Poole, via Wimborne and Cranborne, to Salisbury was constructed in 1755.
Chene Manor is the home of Sir John and Lady Grebe and their daughter Barbara. "One wing showed extreme antiquity, having . . . a kitchen of vast dimensions, in which (it was said) breakfasts had been cooked for John of Gaunt."	Canford Manor was the home of the Webb family during the 17th and 18th centuries. It was considerably enlarged in the 19th century and now forms part of Canford School. The oldest portion is known as John of Gaunt's Kitchen.
Edmond Willowes is "A young fellow of Shottsford-Forum".	Blandford Forum.
Barbara and Edmond meet at the Lornton Inn. It was a "solitary wayside tavern". . .	The Horton Inn occupies a conspicuous roadside position between Wimborne and Cranborne.
After their marriage Barbara and Edmond live at Yewsholt Lodge.	Farr's House at Pamphill near Wimborne.
Knollingwood Hall is the home of the Earl of Uplandtowers, and of his wife Barbara after their marriage.	St Giles House, Wimborne St Giles. Since the 15th century it has belonged to the Ashley-Cooper family who became successive Earls of Shaftesbury from 1672.

(c) *The Marchioness of Stonehenge.* According to Lea, the "classical mansion . . . standing not a hundred miles from the city of Melchester," . . . refers to Wilton House, Wiltshire.

Lady Caroline and her parents live in a classical mansion near Melchester. After a secret, and short, marriage to the assistant land steward, she later marries the Marquis of Stonehenge.	**Wilton House was first built in the 16th century and was enlarged in the 18th century and in 1801. It was granted to the first Earl of Pembroke in 1801.**

(d) *Lady Mottisfont.* Deansleigh Park and Fernell Hall, the two adjoining estates which feature here are identified by Lea as Broadlands and Embley Park, near Romsey in Hampshire.

Sir Ashley Mottisfont marries his second wife Philippa in Wintoncester Cathedral.	**Winchester Cathedral still retains considerable amounts of Norman work, notably in the transepts and crossing.**
Deansleigh Park is the home of Sir Ashley and Philippa. Here they look after a little girl named Dorothy whom Sir Ashley "found one day in a patch of wild oats". . . .	**Broadlands House is of 17th century origin, and was altered and extended in 1767–68 and again in 1788.**
Fernell Hall on the adjoining estate is being leased by an Italian Contessa who seems to have a particular interest in little Dorothy.	**Embley Park in East Wellow parish was largely rebuilt late in the 19th century. It is now a school.**

(e) *The Lady Icenway.* This story takes place during the reign of King George III (1760–1820), and the two houses featured are, according to Lea, Longleat House in Wiltshire and Marwell Hall in Hampshire.

Maria Heymere lives with her uncle in what was described by Leland as "a faire maner-place".	**Longleat House was built in Elizabethan times for Sir John Thynne, to whose descendants it still belongs.**
In due course Maria marries Lord Icenway "whose seat was beyond Wintoncester, quite at t'other end of Wessex".	**Marwell Hall near Winchester was rebuilt in 1816, incorporating portions of the original house. Its grounds now form an extensive zoological park.**

(f) *Squire Petrick's Lady.* Squire Timothy Petrick of Stapleford Park can be readily identified as Peter Walker of Stalbridge House who died in 1745 at the age of 83, from the following extracts from Hutchins 3rd edition. – "Peter Walker would not lend money or buy without seeing every acre: . . . Peter his son died in his life-time, . . . By his will, dated December 26, 1744, he gave this estate, . . . to his eldest grandson Peter,". . .

Old Timothy Petrick was the owner of vast estates, "among them the great manor of Stapleford, on which he lived, in the splendid old mansion now pulled down;". . . .	**Stalbridge House was a fine Elizabethan house demolished in 1822. It is illustrated in the 2nd and 3rd editions of Hutchins.**

(g) *Anna, Lady Baxby.* The basis for this story is to be found in all three editions of Hutchins, concerning the first Parliamentary siege of Sherborne Castle on 2 September 1642. – "While the Earl of Bedford besieged the castle, tradition reports that the wife of George, Lord Digby, . . . his sister, was then at the lodge. He sent a message to desire her to quit it, as he had orders to demolish it. She immediately went on horseback to his tent, at the camp now called Bedford's Castle, and told him, "if he persisted in his intention, he should find his sister's bones buried in the ruins," and instantly left him;". . .

Lady Baxby is virtually alone at Sherton Castle when over 7,000 Parliamentary troops arrive to besiege it. "By a strange freak of destiny", they are under the command of her brother.	**The Norman castle at Sherborne has belonged to the Digby family since 1617. During the Civil Wars it was held for the king, finally being captured on 15 August 1645. It was afterwards blown up.**

(h) *The Lady Penelope*. Here again the real characters upon which this story is based can be readily identified in Hutchins from the pedigree and register entries of the Trenchard family, this extract being concerned with the Wolfeton branch:-

1. Elizabeth Whitson = Sir George Trenchard = 2. Penelope, 2nd
   knighted 1603: died   daughter and coheir
   during his father's   of Lord Darcy. . .*
   life-time (i.e. before 1630)

* A footnote concerning Lady Penelope states:- . . . "Sir George dying soon after his marriage, she remarried Sir John Gage of Firle, c.Sussex, Bart. by whom only she had issue; and being again left a widow she then married Sir William Harvey of Ickworth, Knt. She was courted by her three husbands at one time; but quarrels arising between them, she artfully put an end to them by threatening the first agressor with her perpetual displeasure, and humourously told them that if they would be quiet, and have patience, she would have them all in their turns, which at last actually happened."

Sir George Drenghard lives at a manor house near Casterbridge by the road to Ivell.	**Wolfeton House, Charminster, is mostly of 16th century date. It formerly belonged to the Trenchard family.**

(i) *The Duchess of Hamptonshire*. For some reason, perhaps at Hardy's insistance, the last two noble dames in this series are not referred to by Lea, and there has consequently been some speculation as to the identity of Batton Castle. Unlike the other stories, the characters and buildings here seem to have been drawn from different sources, possibly to make factual inferences more difficult. It has been suggested that Badminton House may have been the model for Batton Castle on account of some similarity of name, but it does not bear any other resemblance to Hardy's description. On the other hand, Lulworth Castle fits the description perfectly, even to the extent of the "stacks of battlemented chimneys" which can be seen in old prints.

Batton Castle "stood in the midst of a park . . . it was a castellated mansion as regular as a chessboard on its ground-plan, ornamented with make-believe bastions and machiolations, behind which were stacks of battlemented chimneys".	**Lulworth Castle, in its parkland setting, is in reality a house designed to resemble a castle. According to Hutchins "The foundations were laid in 1588, and the building was finished 1609. . . It is an exact cube of 80 feet,". . . . It was gutted by fire on 29 August 1929.**

A Group of Noble Dames

(j) *The Honourable Laura.* It is Christmas Eve, and a young couple arrive during a snowstorm at a lonely hotel "standing near the wild north coast of Lower Wessex," . . . about six miles from Cliff-Martin (Coombe Martin).

Lord Quantock's daughter Laura and Signor Smittozzi are eloping and arrive at the Prospect Hotel.	Hunters Inn lies five or six miles east of Coombe Martin. The old inn has been rebuilt since the 19th century.
Laura is already married to Captain Northbrook, the wedding having taken place at St Mary's, Toneborough.	The church of St Mary Magdalene, Taunton, is noted for its magnificent west tower.
Captain Northbrook and Signor Smittozzi go to a nearby beach by way of a "chasm in the cliff" where they intend to fight a duel, but the unscrupulous Smittozzi pushes his opponent over the cliff into a rushing cascade.	At Heddon's Mouth, the valley of the little River Heddon forms a picturesque cutting through the cliffs as it joins the sea. There is a cascade down the cliff at nearby Woody Bay.
Signor Smittozzi plans to take Laura to Cliff-Martin where they can hire a coach to Downstaple.	Coombe Martin, on the north coast of Devonshire, and Barnstaple.

(k) *The Doctor's Legend.* This somewhat macabre story was almost certainly intended to form part of the Group of Noble Dames series, but although published in New York in 1891, it did not appear in this country. Neither the characters nor the locations are given even fictional names, but there can be no doubt that the story refers to Joseph Damer and his notorious removal of the little town of Milton Abbas.

Initially the squire is living at a mansion "not more than half a dozen miles from the Wessex coast". . . .	Winterborne Came House was built for John Damer (brother of Joseph) in 1754.
The squire's wife receives a fright when passing by the churchyard.	Winterborne Came church (see Alicia's Diary).
The squire buys an abbey and its estates, which "stood in a lovely and fertile valley". . . .	Joseph Damer bought the Milton Abbas estate in 1752, and was created Lord Milton in 1753.
"The Abbey was pulled down wing by wing, and a fair mansion built on its site,". . . .	Milton Abbey House was built 1771–76, the architect being Sir William Chambers.
The squire "carted the village bodily away to a distance of a mile, where he built new,". . . .	The 'new' village of Milton Abbas was built c1780, and it is one of the earliest examples of a planned village.

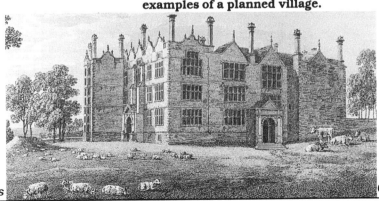

The former Stalbridge House. An engraving of 1813 by J. Emes which appears in the 2nd and 3rd editions of Hutchins. The house was demolished in 1822.

28. Tess of the d'Urbervilles

PARSON TRINGHAM'S account of the fictional d'Urbervilles is essentially that of Hutchins who states that the factual Turbervilles descended from a certain Sir Payne de Turberville who came from Normandy in 1066. Branches of the family later became established in several parts of the country, including Bere Regis where they were successive lords of the manor for some 500 years, from early in the 13th century until the male line became extinct in 1710. The south aisle of Bere Regis church was their family chapel, where memorials to them still remain, together with a burial vault beneath the floor. This family was once powerful, influential and numerous, particularly during the early 16th century when offshoots from the Bere Regis branch became established at Wool and Winterborne Whitechurch. Such extinction of a once great family seems to have held a particular fascination for Hardy who developed it as a theme for this great and still popular novel.

Lea is insistent that Talbothayes dairy farm is not based upon any particular place, being merely typical of many such farms in the Frome valley, but as it plays such an important part in the novel, there have inevitably been attempts to identify it more specifically. The name comes from a real property, which belonged to the Hardy family, lying half a mile east of West Stafford, but it has never been a dairy farm. Norris Mill Farm and Woodsford Castle have been claimed as models for the fictional Talbothayes dairy, but Denys Kay-Robinson's suggestion of Lower Lewell Farm seems more likely on several counts. The buildings more nearly fit Hardy's description, it lies close to the real Talbothayes, and when the girls go by way of the flooded lane to Mellstock church, it is said to have involved a walk of three or four miles. Perhaps another clue is that one of the milk-men at Talbothayes is named Bill Lewell.

John Durbeyfield says – "There's a very pretty brew in tap at The Pure Drop"...	The Crown, Marnhull, is a fine old 17th century inn of stone and thatch.
The village of Marlott "lay amid the north-eastern undulations of the beautiful Vale of Blakemore or Blackmoor"...	The Blackmore Vale, covering a large part of north Dorset, is bordered on the south by a series of steep-sided chalk hills.
John Durbeyfield, his wife Joan, their eldest daughter Tess and their six other children live in an old cottage at Marlott.	'Tess Cottage', Marnhull. Hardy is said to have visited it in later life, inferring that the Durbeyfield's cottage had been based upon it.
Tess had attended the village school at Marlott.	Marnhull School was built in 1874 and enlarged in 1883.
The Durbeyfields' local is 'Rollivers' where the regulars use an upstairs bedroom as an unofficial bar.	Probably the Blackmoor Vale Inn at Marnhull which has been partially rebuilt since the 19th century.
On her way to Casterbridge, Tess "passed the little town of Stourcastle,"...	Sturminster Newton, where several thatched houses still remain in the lower part near the river.

Later she can see "the elevation called Bulbarrow . . . well-nigh the highest in South Wessex . . . engirdled by its earthen trenches".

Bulbarrow, at 902 feet is the second highest hill in Dorset. On the west side is the Iron Age hill-fort of Rawlsbury.

Tess walks to "the hill-town called Shaston", where she boards a carrier's van.

Shaftesbury, a unique hill-top town, was one of the four Dorset boroughs at the time of the Domesday survey of 1086.

She arrives at Trantridge where she is to work for the Stoke d'Urbervilles.

Pentridge is a small secluded village three miles north east of Cranborne.

John Durbeyfield has inherited from his ancestors "an old seal marked with a ramping lion on a shield, and a castle over him".

The arms of the Bere Regis Turbervilles were:- Ermine, a lion rampant, crowned gules: crest a castle argent.

Tess waits for her friends at 'The Flower-de-Luce' at Chaseborough.

The Fleur-de-Lis at Cranborne is of 16th century origin.

She is carried off on horseback by Alec d'Urberville into "The Chase – the oldest wood in England" . . .

Cranborne Chase, once more densely wooded, was a famous hunting ground for kings and nobles.

Tess visits the vicar of Marlott concerning the baptism of her illegitimate baby son.

The old rectory at Marnhull, opposite the church has a datestone of 1695.

Her baby is buried in a shabby corner of the churchyard.

The parish church of St Gregory at Marnhull.

Tess travels southwards to the fertile Froom valley, known as the 'Valley of the Great Dairies'.

The Frome valley is bounded by heathland for much of its length eastwards from Dorchester.

She arrives at Talbothayes Dairy where she is engaged in milking for the busy summer season.

Lower Lewell Farm comprises several old buildings, including a 17th century farmhouse, 18th century dairy-house and a thatched barn of 1704.

When the butter fails to 'come', Dairyman Crick recalls, "My grandfather used to go to Conjuror Mynterne, out at Owlscombe," . . .

At Batcombe, the Minternes were at one time lords of the manor, one of them being known as 'Conjuror Minterne'.

One Sunday the milkmaids go to church at Mellstock, "three or four miles distant". . .

Stinsford church (see Under the Greenwood Tree).

Emminster is the home town of Angel Clare, a farming student at Talbothayes.

The little west Dorset town of Beaminster.

Angel visits his parents at Emminster, where his father is the vicar.

The Old Vicarage off Clay Lane, Beaminster, is now a guest house.

Whilst driving the farm wagon to a railway station, Angel points out to Tess an old manor house which once belonged to the d'Urbervilles.

Evidently they passed within sight of Woolbridge Manor, so that their destination was presumably Wool station.

Angel Clare next intends to study milling at the Wellbridge flour mills.

Bindon Mill was once run by the monks of Bindon Abbey. The mediaeval buildings were rebuilt in 1770.

Angel Clare and Tess are married in the parish church which is "a long way off,". . .

Lower Lewell Farm is situated in West Knighton parish, some 1 ½ miles from the village and church.

After their marriage they stay at Wellbridge, in an old farmhouse which once was "a fine manorial residence . . . of a d'Urberville,". . . . It stood by a "great Elizabethan bridge". . .

Woolbridge Manor House at Wool adjoins a fine old 16th century bridge over the Frome. The house is of early 17th century date and formerly belonged to a branch of the Turberville family.

Retty Priddle and Marian went to Lew-Everard, "where they had summut to drink,". . .

The Everard family once owned West Stafford where the inn is The Wise Man.

Later they parted at Dree-armed Cross, after which Retty tried to drown herself in the Great Pool.

The three-way road junction north-west of West Stafford, and one of the local weirs, probably that at Woodsford (see *The Return of the Native*). 'Dree' is the Dorset word for 'three'.

Whilst sleep-walking, Angel carries Tess across a narrow footbridge into the nearby abbey ruins.

Bindon Abbey was founded in 1149 at Bindon Hill near Lulworth, and moved to the Wool site in 1172.

Angel lays Tess in "the empty stone coffin of an abbot . . . in the ruined choir of the Abbey-church."

A 13th century stone coffin of an abbot still remains in the choir area of the abbey remains.

Angel and Tess leave Wellbridge and travel northwards by way of Weatherbury and Stagfoot Lane where they rest a while at the Lane Inn before finally parting.

Leaving Wool via Puddletown and Hartfoot Lane, an older name for the village of Melcombe Bingham. The site of the original Fox Inn at the corner of Cothayes Drove is now occupied by a pair of cottages having a stone inscribed 'OLD FOX 1947'.

Tess seeks Marian at Flintcomb-Ash, which is "a farm near Nettlecombe Tout". . .

Nettlecombe Tout is a prominent hill forming part of the northern escarpment of the Dorset chalklands, half-a-mile east of Folly.

"Before her, in a slight depression, were the remains of a village. She had, in fact, reached Flintcomb-Ash, . . . At the entrance to the village was a cottage whose gable jutted into the road."

The small village of Plush, north-east of Piddletrenthide, where the gable of a cottage adjoins the roadside.

Tess commences winter work at the upland farm – "'Tis a starve-acre place. Corn and swedes are all they grow."

Church Hill in Alton Pancras parish, north of Plush. There is a prehistoric earthwork enclosure on the bleak upland.

On her journey to Emminster, Tess passes Dogbury and High Stoy Hills and "the dell between them called The Devil's Kitchen".

The valley between Dogbury Hill and High Stoy comprises Lyon's Gate and Dogbury Gate.

At Evershead she has breakfast "at a cottage by the church".

'Tess Cottage' at Evershot stands just to the west of the church.

Tess continues "through a more gentle country, by way of Benvill Lane".

Benville Lane lies between Evershot and Toller Down Gate on the A356.

At Emminster, Tess reaches the church as the congregation are coming out.

Beaminster church is noted for its magnificent early 16th century west tower.

On her return journey Tess finds Alec d'Urberville preaching in a barn at Evershead.

A former barn in Tannery Lane, Evershot, now demolished.

Tess and Alec d'Urberville stop by the Cross-in-Hand. A shepherd says "'Tis a thing of ill-omen, Miss".

The roadside stone on Batcombe Hill, known as the Cross and Hand, is possibly of Saxon origin.

Alec d'Urberville goes off "in the direction of Abbot's-Cernel".

Cerne Abbas is an ancient Dorset village clustered around the remains of a former great abbey.

Returning to Marlott, Tess passes the village inn at Nuttlebury.

The Antelope Inn at Hazelbury Bryan.

She imagines the sleeping inhabitants of Nuttlebury rising at the first signs of dawn over Hambledon Hill.

Hambledon Hill is an Iron Age hill-fort lying to the east of Child Okeford.

After John Durbeyfield's death the family leave Marlott and move to Kingsbere. They approach by way of "an eminence . . . called Greenhill".

Woodbury Hill is an Iron Age hill-fort near Bere Regis, which was the site of an annual fair for more than 800 years.

"Under the hill, . . . was the half-dead townlet of . . . Kingsbere," . . . the home of their ancestors.

Bere Regis, where the Turberville family had been lords of the manor for some 500 years.

At Kingsbere, no lodgings are available, and all their household goods are unloaded against the churchyard wall.

The old pound wall at Bere Regis, adjoining the churchyard is built mainly of stonework from the former manor house.

The Durbeyfields set up camp by the south wall of the church under "a beautiful traceried window, . . . called the d'Urberville window," . . .

The Turberville window in the south aisle of Bere Regis church is of c1536, the stained glass featuring arms of the Turberville family being of 1875.

Nearby could be seen "the green foundations . . . where the d'Urberville mansion once had stood," . . .

The former manor house of the Turbervilles which stood in Court Green to the east of the church was demolished early in the 19th century.

Alec d'Urberville is staying at an inn at Kingsbere.

Probably the Royal Oak, Bere Regis.

Tess goes into the church and looks at the ancient and crumbling d'Urberville tombs "their brasses torn from the matrices, the rivet-holes remaining like martin-holes in a sand-cliff".

Two 16th century Purbeck marble table-tomb memorials of the Turbervilles remain in the south aisle of Bere Regis church. The memorial brasses have long been missing, probably since the Civil Wars.

Tess reads the inscription on "the door of her ancestral sepulchre," . . .

The worn inscription on the floor slab of the Turberville vault is in both Latin and English.

In the dusk Tess passes "near an altar-tomb, the oldest of them all, on which was a recumbent figure". . . . It is actually the live figure of Alec d'Urberville.

The oldest of the Turberville table-tombs, of the early 14th century, lies under a cusped recess in the south wall of the south aisle.

Angel Clare, who has returned from abroad, finds Tess at a lodging-house in Sandbourne.

Bournemouth had become a fashionable seaside resort by the late 19th century.

Angel and Tess flee into the New Forest and spend several days in an empty house named Bramshurst Court.

Moyles Court, a 17th century house north of Ringwood, is now a school.

The fugitives unavoidably pass through Melchester in order to cross a large river by way of the "town bridge".

St Nicholas Bridge, Salisbury, built in 1245, was the main southern entry to the city until Harnham Bridge was opened in 1933.

Tess is arrested at dawn at Stonehenge.

Stonehenge—the most spectacular prehistoric monument in Britain.

In the final scene, Angel Clare and Tess's sister 'Liza-Lu are leaving Wintoncester, where a black flag hoisted above the prison signifies that an execution has just taken place.

The ancient city of Winchester was once the capital of the kingdom of Wessex.

The Turberville window in the south aisle of Bere Regis church.

Tess of the d'Urbervilles

29.   A Few Crusted Characters

THE CARRIER'S van for Upper Longpuddle (Piddletrenthide) is just leaving Casterbridge when a latecomer hails them and climbs aboard. Although apparently a stranger, he proves to be an old Longpuddle resident returning after a long period abroad, and his enquiries as to the fate of other old residents of the village prompts a series of reminiscences by the passengers as they jog along homeward.

The carrier's van for Upper Longpuddle leaves from the White Hart in the county town.

The White Hart Hotel stands at the bottom of High East Street, Dorchester. On market days its forecourt was thronged with carrier's vans.

Preparations for departure are already under way when it is "half-past three by the clock in the turret at the top of the street".

The Dorchester Corn Exchange was rebuilt in 1848, but the corner clock turret was a later addition, completed in December 1863.

Cousins Steve and James Hardcome and their wives go for their annual summer outing to Budmouth-Regis which they reach by train from Casterbridge, "the line being just opened"

Weymouth station was opened in January 1857 on completion of the Yeovil to Weymouth line.

At Budmouth, Stephen Hardcome and his cousin's wife are drowned whilst rowing in the bay. Their bodies are brought back to Upper Longpuddle and buried in the churchyard.

Piddletrenthide church is of Norman origin, but was mostly rebuilt during the 15th century. The fine west tower is dated 1487.

An apparition of old William Privett has been seen to enter Longpuddle church . . . "on Midsummer Night it is believed hereabouts that the faint shapes of all the folk who are going to be at death's door within the year can be seen entering the church". . .

The south doorway of Piddletrenthide church is a fine Norman one through which generations of villagers have passed for more than 800 years.

Parson Toogood of Scrimpton always dines at the Squire's house on the occasion of family Christenings.

The former squires of Frampton were the Sheridans of Frampton Court which stood to the south west of the village.

Andrey Satchel arrives at Scrimpton church for his wedding in a drunken state, and he and his bride are locked in the tower out of sight until Andrey sobers up.

Frampton church has an unusual west tower. It was built in 1695 to replace an earlier one which had collapsed, and has superimposed Tuscan columns at the angles.

Meanwhile Parson Toogood returns to his house.

Frampton Rectory is a fine 18th century house.

Parson Toogood and his manservant impulsively join a hunting party, riding across country as far as Yalbury Wood. In the excitement Andrey and his bride are completely forgotten.

Yellowham Wood is a large tract of heathy woodland between Dorchester and Puddletown.

During Christmas week it was the custom in Longpuddle for the church band and choirboys to go to the manor-house "to play and sing . . . to the squire's people and visitors".

Old Andrey Satchel (father of Andrey in the previous tale) "knew no more of music than the Giant o' Cernel;" . . . but he goes along to the manor-house with the rest of the church band, posing as a violinist.

George Crookhill is travelling home from Melchester and meets up with a stranger on the road. "When they came to Woodyates Inn they stopped . . . and agreed to drink together;". . .

The manor house at Piddletrenthide is an 18th century building on the site of an earlier one. The upper storey was added in 1832.

The Cerne Giant, Dorset's renowned chalk-cut hill-figure of a naked man with a club, is thought to date from Roman times and to represent Hercules.

The former Woodyates Inn was a famous coaching inn half-way between Salisbury and Blandford, where King George III changed horses and dined on his way to Weymouth.

Piddletrenthide manor house.

The Norman south doorway of Piddletrenthide church.

The former Woodyates Inn, Pentridge. Drawing based on an etching and old photographs.

A Few Crusted Characters

30   The Son's Veto

SOPHY, A parlourmaid, marries her employer, The Reverend Twycott, after the death of his first wife. Because of Sophy's lack of social standing they move to London, but later their son, who has had a public school education, becomes very aware of his mother's educational shortcomings, particularly after she becomes a widow.

Sophy is parlourmaid at Gaymead vicarage, the home of the Rev. Twycott who becomes a widower at a relatively early age.

Lea identifies the village of Gaymead as Shinfield on the south side of Reading. The vicarage lies near the church.

Sophy and the Rev. Twycott are married in Gaymead church.

The parish church at Shinfield is of 13th century origin.

Sam Hobson, formerly the gardener at Gaymead vicarage, eventually has his own fruiterer's shop in Aldbrickham.

Reading, the largest town in Berkshire, features more particularly in *Jude the Obscure.*

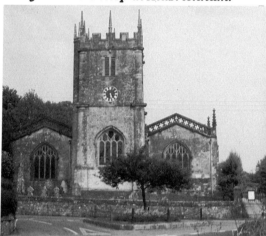

Frampton church and rectory, and right, the former Frampton Court, a photolithograph from John Pouncy's Dorset Photographically Illustrated *(1857). These three buildings feature in* A Few Crusted Characters *(see page 73).*

31. For Conscience Sake

MR MILLBORNE of Toneborough (Taunton) deserted his fiancee Leonora and moved away to London, despite the fact that she subsequently bore him a daughter Frances. Now, twenty years later, his conscience is still troubling him, and having discovered that they are living in Exonbury (Exeter), he resolves to visit them with a view to a somewhat belated marriage.

Frances is engaged to the Rev. Percival Cope who is curate at St John's church, Ivell.

The fine parish church of St John, Yeovil, was rebuilt late in the 14th century.

The Millbornes, now married, "spend a week at a watering place in the Isle of Wight".

The Isle of Wight still remains a popular venue for holidays and excursions.

Mr Millborne arranges for Leonora and Frances to live at "a little old manor-house . . . standing a mile from Mr Cope's town of Ivell".

Newton Surmaville is a manor house, built between 1602 and 1612, and situated about a mile south-east of Yeovil.

The beautiful early 17th century manor house of Newton Surmaville, near Yeovil, Somerset.

32. On the Western Circuit

CHARLES RAYE is a lawyer, and whilst in Melchester (Salisbury) meets a young servant girl, Anna, at a fair. Due to the travelling involved in Charles' profession their subsequent romance is carried on largely by correspondence, but as poor Anna can neither read nor write, she is assisted by her employer, Mrs Edith Harman.

Charles Raye is standing in the Close in the city of Melchester when he is attracted by the sounds of a fair in the city square.

The Close at Salisbury contains many fine buildings forming an appropriate setting for one of the most beautiful of English cathedrals.

The house of Anna's employer is situated near a corner of the city square, and is a "dignified residence of considerable size, having several windows on each floor".

There is a house of this description on the east side of Salisbury city square, at the beginning of Queen Street. The ground floor now comprises shops.

Edith Harman attends the "usual week-day service in Melchester cathedral", where she sees Charles Raye again.

The foundation stones of Salisbury cathedral were laid in 1220 and the building was consecrated in 1258.

On the day after the fair, Charles and Anna "walked out of the city . . . to the earthworks of Old Melchester,". . .

Old Sarum has been successively an Iron Age hill-fort, the Roman station of Sorviodunum, and Norman cathedral city. It was abandoned in the 13th century in favour of the new site at Salisbury, or New Sarum.

When not in Melchester, Anna stays with friends at a cottage on the Plain.

Salisbury Plain covers a large area of Wiltshire north west of Salisbury.

After their marriage Charles and Anna spend their honeymoon at Knollsea.

Swanage (see *The Hand of Ethelberta*).

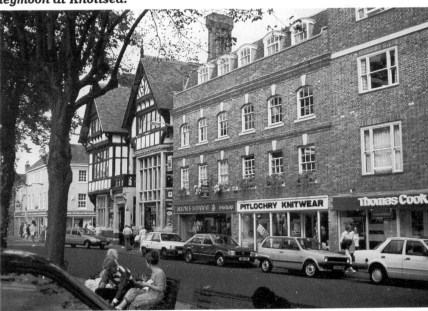

An 18th century house near the north-east corner of the city square, in Queen Street, Salisbury, Wiltshire.

33. To Please His Wife

CAPTAIN SHADRACH Jolliffe returns to his home town of Havenpool (Poole) after a long and hazardous voyage, and there marries Joanna, one of two former sweethearts. They settle down quietly with a small grocery business, but Joanna is envious of the other girl Emily who has married a wealthy merchant and lives in a large house across the street.

Shadrach Jolliffe goes into St James' church to offer a prayer of thanksgiving for deliverance from shipwreck.

The parish church of St James, Poole, was totally rebuilt in 1820 during the incumbency of the Rev. P.W. Joliffe.

Captain Jolliffe is able to see "the harbour and the island beyond" . . . from his lodgings.

Poole Harbour is the second largest natural harbour in the world. Brownsea is the largest of its islands.

Shadrach and Joanna pass the Town Hall as they walk towards her home.

The Guildhall, Poole, with its distinctive external stairs, was built in 1761.

After their marriage Shadrach and Joanna "take on a small grocers' shop in High Street,". . .

Poole High Street, the main shopping street of the town, has undergone considerable changes in recent years.

Emily marries a prosperous merchant and they live in a "large, substantial brick mansion" which faced directly on the High Street,". . .

Number 100, High Street Poole, was a substantial 18th century brick merchant's house, which in later years became Barclay's Bank. It is still in the same ownership, but has been totally rebuilt in ashlar stone.

When Shadrach and their two sons have not returned from their voyage after almost two years, Joanna often watches "on the hill behind the port,". . .

Constitution Hill was formerly a high view point on the heath outside the town, but it is now absorbed into the general conurbation of Poole and Parkstone.

When indoors, Joanna's hopes are raised on hearing "a shout or excitement . . . at the corner of the Town Cellar, where the High Street joined the Quay,". . .

The 15th century Town Cellars is Poole's oldest building. It has served a number of purposes in the past including warehouse and town jail. It is now a maritime museum.

Poole High Street. A print of 1870 from Newman & Co's Illustrations of British Scenery. Source: Rodney Legg collection.

To Please His Wife

34. The Well-Beloved

THE ISLE of Slingers (Portland) is referred to in several of the Wessex novels, but here it is almost exclusively the setting for this innovative story. Jocelyn Pierston, a native of the island, is a successful sculptor living and working in London, whose artistic nature is constantly seeking an elusive ideal in womanhood, which seems to flit inexplicably from one female form to another. This ideal image manifests itself most strongly in three successive generations of island girls – Avice Caro, her daughter Ann Avice, and grand-daughter Avice – but each time the affair is destined to end just short of marriage. There is a twenty year generation gap between each of the three episodes, the first being at a time when the Budmouth railway station "had only recently been opened". The line from Yeovil to Weymouth was opened in January 1857, so that the three episodes can be regarded as set in c1857, 1877, and 1897.

Jocelyn is returning to his native Isle of Slingers, "that Gibraltar of Wessex", which is "connected to the mainland by a long thin neck of pebbles".

Dorset's unique offshore Chesil Beach stretches for almost ten miles from Abbotsbury to Portland, its pebbles forming a tenuous link with the mainland.

In the opening scene he is climbing the steep road through the "sea-skirted townlet definable as the Street of Wells".

Fortuneswell, now the principal town on Portland, originated and rapidly grew during the 19th century.

Jocelyn and Avice walk "to the southern part of the island called the Beal, . . . pausing over the treacherous cavern known as Cave Hole,". . .

Cave Hole lies on the eastern coast of the island, near Portland Bill. Boats have been driven into it. One can look down into it through cracks in the coastal path which become blow-holes in an easterly gale.

Walking home at night, Jocelyn and Avice hear the sound of the sea in "the vast concave of Deadman's Bay,". . .

Lyme Bay stretches from Portland to Start Point on the south coast of Devon. In the days of sail, many ships were wrecked on its shores.

Jocelyn and Avice go to "the old Hope Churchyard which lay in a ravine formed by a landslip ages ago".

The ruins of Portland's old parish church of St Andrew still remain near the edge of the cliffs above Church Ope Cove.

Jocelyn is returning to London, and Avice plans to accompany him across the Chesil Beach "as far as to Henry the Eighth's Castle above the sands,". . .

Sandsfoot Castle on the mainland was built in 1541, being one of a series of King Henry VIII's coastal forts.

Leaving the island, Jocelyn passes "the ruins of the village destroyed by the November gale of 1824,". . .

The great storm of 23 November 1824 caused havoc along the Dorset coast, particularly at Fleet and at Chiswell on Portland where 30 people were drowned in their homes.

Jocelyn and Marcia Bencomb, walking along the Chesil Beach towards Budmouth, "reached a precarious wood bridge,". . .

Portland was reached by ferry across the mouth of the Fleet at Smallmouth until 1839 when the first wooden Ferrybridge was built.

20 years later, Jocelyn again returns to the island. Since his last visit the railway has been constructed, and he is able to make the journey from Budmouth by train.

The line from Weymouth to Portland was opened in 1865, the main station being at Victoria Square, Fortuneswell.

Jocelyn arrives in time to see the funeral of the first Avice taking place in the churchyard, and later meets her daughter Ann Avice.

The church of St George at Reforne, Portland, was built in 1754–64, and is set in a large churchyard with row upon row of Portland gravestones.

Ann Avice continues to live in her mother's cottage near Sylvania Castle.

The thatched 'Avice's Cottage' at Wakeham has a 1640 datestone and now forms part of the Portland Museum.

Jocelyn moves into Sylvania Castle which he is renting for the summer months. It is "a dignified manor-house . . . with modern castellations and battlements".

Pennsylvania Castle, Portland, was designed by James Wyatt and built in 1800 for John Penn, Governor of Portland and grandson of William Penn the founder of Pennsylvania.

Jocelyn visits "the Red King's castle overhanging the cliff, beside whose age the castle he occupied was but a thing of yesterday."

Rufus Castle above Church Ope Cove, Portland, was originally a motte and bailey castle reputedly built during the reign of William Rufus (1087–1100). The present ruined building is of the late 15th century.

Mrs Pine-Avon attends the parish church on Sunday, and Jocelyn "took a seat behind her".

The original 18th century box pews, pulpit and other internal fittings still remain complete in St George's church.

Jocelyn follows Ann Avice to the military fortifications. "Above them towered the grey-green mountain of grassy stone, here levelled at the top by military art."

The Verne, Portland. In 1860 work was begun on converting this natural stronghold into a huge military fort, with a large dry moat and earth covered ramparts.

Jocelyn chances to meet his old friend Somers and his family "on the Budmouth Esplanade".

Weymouth esplanade continued to be a favourite promenade for holiday-makers in the 1890s.

The third Avice and Henri Leverre go to the Cove, from where they plan to row a boat to Budmouth.

Church Ope Cove, on the east side of Portland, was the main landing place for the island fishermen.

They reach the Cove by way of a narrow lane which passed under the old castle arch.

The arched footbridge to Rufus Castle still spans the footpath which runs between Avice's Cottage and Church Ope Cove.

They launch the boat without oars, and are in danger of being carried by the tide into the Race.

The Race is a very rough patch of water off Portland Bill where contra-flowing tidal currents meet.

The Well-Beloved

35. The Fiddler of the Reels

WAT OLLAMOOR, otherwise known as "Mop" by reason of his hairstyle, is a talented violinist whose exceptional virtuosity produces an irresistible urge to dance on any who come within earshot of the strains of his fiddle. Young Car'line Aspent of Stickleford (Tincleton) is particularly susceptible to his influence in this respect, and in others. The date of this short story is set between the opening of the railway from Southampton to Dorchester in 1847 and the Great Exhibition of 1851, so that the period is similar to that of *Under the Greenwood Tree* and *The Return of the Native*. Several of the locations also occur in these two earlier novels and need not be repeated in this section. They include Mellstock Bridge (Bockhampton Bridge) and Mop's lodgings nearby, the Quiet Woman Inn, Mistover, Stickleford and Bloom's End.

Mop Ollamoor goes to visit a "woman whom he spoke of as his Intended, and who lived at Moreford,". . .

Moreton is a secluded village on the borders of the heath and the Frome valley.

Ned Hipcroft, Car'lines original fiancé, has been working in London on "the huge glass-house in Hyde Park".

The Crystal Palace, Joseph Paxton's innovative building built for the Great Exhibition of 1851.

Car'line and her little girl are walking from Casterbridge to Stickleford. "In the course of three miles they had passed Heedless-William's Pond, the familiar landmark by Bloom's End," . . .

The lane from Stinsford Hill, above Dorchester, to Tincleton. Heedless William's Pond, about half a mile east of Bockhampton Cross, is said to be named after a certain William, a reckless coachman who swerved off the road into the pond and was drowned.

Bockhampton Bridge, Stinsford, which also features in Under the Greenwood Tree *(page 15) and Heedless William's Pond. Recent research by C.L. Sinclair Williams (DNHAS Proceedings, vol. 110, pp 161-163) shows the name to have been in use as long ago as 1372, the original form being probably 'Headless William' and referring to the still existing roadside stone nearby, rather than to the pond.*

36.   An Imaginative Woman

THE MARCHMILL family are on holiday at Solentsea in Upper Wessex. The lodgings they take are normally occupied by a young poet who is temporarily away, and although Mrs Marchmill has never met him, she is familiar with his poems, and takes an exceptional interest in his photograph.

The Marchmill family arrive in Solentsea for their holiday, and take up lodgings on New Parade.

The seaside resort of Southsea now forms part of the general conurbation of Portsmouth.

The poet Robert Trewe has left his lodgings in Solentsea for a while, and is staying at "a little cottage on the island opposite,". . .

The Isle of Wight, on the other side of the water from Southsea. The offshore anchorage is known as Spithead and the main channel to the west is The Solent.

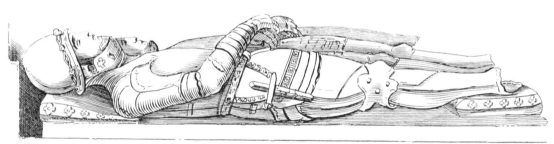

Monumental figures of Sir John Horsey & his Son.

The recumbent effigies of Sir John Horsey and his son Sir John in Sherborne Abbey Church. Engraving from Hutchins 2nd edition, volume 4 (1815). Sir John junior is the subject of the short story erroneously titled Master John Horseleigh, Knight (page 83).

Clifton House, Clifton Maybank, formerly the home of the Horsey family. The south front shown in the photograph retains some 16th century features re-used in the rebuilding of 1786.

An Imaginative Woman

37. Master John Horseleigh, Knight

THIS SHORT story is based on an entry of 1539 in the Poole parish register, and it is evident that Hardy quoted from Hutchins 3rd edition (volume 1, p.50) where the transcription begins:-

"Mastr. John Horssey, Knyght, of the p'ysshe of Clyffton". . . . Unfortunately Hutchins' editors omitted six vital words, for the actual entry in the parish register states:-

"Mastr. John Horssey the Sonn of Sr. John Horssey knyghte of the pyshe of Clyffton wase maryd to Edyth Stocker the wyffe late off John Stocker mchawnte of Pole the xiiii Day of Decmber the pvylegge gevyn by owr supeme hedd of the chyrche of Ingelond kynge Henry the viiith."

Master John Horsey was not therefore a knight at the time of his marriage in 1539, and would not have become one until after his father's death in 1546. Hardy rightly points out that this marriage is not referred to in the Horsey family pedigree, as reproduced in Hutchin's, where John Horsey is recorded as having married Edith, daughter of Richard Phelips of Montacute. However, the identical Christian names are suggestive, and the matter can be resolved by reference to the Addenda to the Herald's Visitation of Dorsetshire of 1623, where a similar pedigree includes the additional note that Edith, the daughter of Richard Phelips was also the widow of John Stocker of Poole.

Hardy's story is based upon a supposed legend that John Horsey had two 'wives' living in different areas, which he lived with in turn, flitting secretly from one to the other, whereas in reality Edith Phelips and Edith Stocker were one and the same person. The wording of the opening paragraph of the story suggests that it might have been originally intended as one of the Group of Noble Dames series.

The narrator quotes a marriage entry of 1539 from the Havenpool parish register concerning John Horseleigh of Clyfton Horseleigh, and refers to the family pedigree.	Sir John Horsey of Clifton Maybank, the subject of this story, who died in 1564, and his father Sir John, who died in 1546, are commemorated by a memorial with their recumbent effigies in Sherborne abbey church.
Edith lives at Oozewood, a small town by the South Avon in Upper Wessex, on the edge of the forest.	Ringwood, Hampshire, lies in the valley of the River Avon, on the western edge of the New Forest.
John Horseleigh's family home is at Clifton Horseleigh, "a mansion which . . . was one of the best known in the county at that time".	Clifton House at Clifton Maybank, built c1550, was one of the finest houses in Dorset, but it was mostly taken down in 1786 when the porch and associated features were re-erected at Montacute.
Edith's brother is told that Master John Horseleigh's wife is "the daughter of Master Richard Phelipson, of Montislope, in Nether Wessex,". . .	Montacute House was built in 1580–1601 for Edward Phelips, speaker of the House of Commons, and Master of the Rolls.

38. Jude the Obscure

ALTHOUGH THE treatment of marriage and divorce in *Jude the Obscure* would not generally be regarded as sensational at the present time, it outraged the strict moral views of the Victorian readers of the 1890s, and so much adverse criticism greeted its publication that Hardy wrote no further novels. The setting is mainly North Wessex, featuring Christminster (Oxford), a seat of learning which Jude regards as a kind of Holy City representing all his ambitions to become a classical linguist and theologian, but his enthusiasm and self-taught knowledge are insufficient to overcome the insuperable obstacles of his humble and poor origins. He is destined to remain a stonemason, and his academic failure has a parallel in his marital affairs, said to be attributable to an unfortunate family trait which is shared by his cousin, Sue Bridehead.

Jude Fawley lives with his great aunt at Marygreen in North Wessex, and one of his chores is to draw water from the well on the village green.

The village of Fawley near Wantage in Berkshire. Hardy's paternal grandmother Mary Head lived at Fawley as a girl. It was formerly called Great Fawley, to distinguish it from South Fawley which is a mile away, but is now known simply as Fawley.

Richard Phillotson, the schoolmaster is leaving Marygreen, much to everyone's regret, particularly Jude's.

The former village school still remains at Fawley.

The cart carrying the schoolmaster's belongings "creaked across the green, and disappeared round the corner by the rectory-house".

The old vicarage at Fawley.

The original church at Marygreen had been demolished. "In place of it a tall new building of modern Gothic design, . . . had been erected on a new piece of ground by a certain obliterator of historic records who had run down from London and back in a day."

The parish church of St Mary at Fawley was totally rebuilt on a new site in 1863, the architect being George Edmund Street of London. He was also responsible for St Peter's which was the first town centre church in Bournemouth and has its Hardy mention in *The Hand of Ethelberta*.

Jude walks to the downs north of Marygreen as far as a green ridgeway which "ran east and west for many miles,". . .

An ancient trackway, the Ridge Way, runs from east to west across the downs about two miles north of Fawley.

From the roof of a nearby barn known as the Brown House, Jude can just discern the city of Christminster in the distance.

A former isolated barn on the downs, known as the Red House, has since been demolished.

Jude begins work as an apprentice stonemason at nearby Alfredston.

Wantage is famous for having been the birthplace of King Alfred (849–900, reigned from 871).

Jude first meets Arabella Donn as he passes by her father's homestead at Cresscombe.	Letcome Bassett, Oxfordshire, where a cottage is known locally as 'Arabella's Cottage'. The village was formerly in Berkshire, until 1974, and noted for its watercress beds.
During their courtship, Jude and Arabella walk on the downs and visit a "circular British earth-bank,". . .	Segsbury Camp or Castle is an Iron Age hill-fort near the Ridge Way on the downs north of Fawley, in the parish of Letcombe Regis which is now in Oxfordshire.
After their marriage they move into a roadside cottage between Marygreen and Alfredston.	A former cottage between Fawley and Wantage, since demolished.
Jude approaches Christminster. "Grey stoned and dun-roofed, it stood within hail of the Wessex border,". . .	Oxford, a beautiful city dominated by the 'dreaming spires' of its churches and colleges.
From Jude's lodging he is able to see the spire of the "Cathedral-church of Cardinal College". . . .	Oxford Cathedral forms part of Christ Church College which was founded by Cardinal Wolsey and known originally as Cardinal College.
Jude sees Sue Bridehead whilst helping to unload stone "outside Crozier College in Old-time Street,". . .	Oriel College, Oxford, was founded in 1326.
Jude sometimes attends "the ceremonial church of St Silas, ". . . near his lodgings in a suburb of the city known as 'Beersheba'.	The church of St Barnabas, completed in 1869 in the Jericho district of Oxford was designed by A.W. Blomfield for whom Hardy worked as an architectural assistant 1862–67.
Jude and Sue arrange to meet "at the cross in the pavement which marked the spot of the Martyrdoms".	The spot in Broad Street where the protestant bishops Latimer and Ridley and archbishop Cranmer were burnt at the stake in 1555 and 1556.
Jude and Sue visit Mr Phillotson who is now teaching at Lumsdon. "Presently the embattled tower and square turret of the church rose into the sky,". . .	Cumnor, a village lying about three miles south-west of Oxford. The parish church of St Michael is of Norman origin, with later mediaeval extensions.
Jude goes up "to an octagonal chamber in the lantern of a singularly built theatre,". . .	The Sheldonian Theatre, Oxford, is a striking circular building designed by Wren, and built in 1664.
Jude wanders about the streets "till be came to a spot called The Fourways in the middle of the city,". . .	The junction of Oxford High Street and St Aldate's Street is known as Carfax.
On his way home Jude goes by way of Biblioll College, where he chalks a text on the wall.	One wing of Balliol College, known as 'Fisher's Building' was built at the expense of Henry Fisher, vicar of Bere Regis 1725-73.
Jude moves to Melchester where he hopes to get work on the restoration of the cathedral.	Salisbury Cathedral (see previous sections). Considerable restoration works were carried out c1870.

Sue Bridehead is at the teacher training-school in the Close at Melchester. "It was an ancient edifice of the fifteenth century, once a palace, now a training-school, with mullioned and transomed windows,". . .

The 15th century King's House in the Close at Salisbury was used as a teacher training college from 1851 until 1978. It is now a museum. Hardy's two sisters attended the college at one time.

Jude and Sue visit Wardour Castle. "They reached the Park and Castle and wandered through the picture-galleries,". . .

Wardour Castle, completed in 1776, lies near the ruins of Old Wardour Castle. It stands beside a lake and became the Cranborne Chase School in 1960.

Jude and Sue go into the empty market-house at Melchester where he tells of his marriage to Arabella.

The public library on the west side of Salisbury square was built in 1973–75 and incorporates the facade of the former market house.

Sue and Richard Phillotson are married at Melchester in "a grey Perpendicular church . . . the church of St Thomas."

The church of St Thomas of Canterbury at Salisbury is mostly of the 15th century.

Having returned to Christminster, Jude visits "a popular tavern", where to his surprise, Arabella is one of the barmaids.

The Lamb and Flag inn forms part of St John's College, Oxford, the lamb and flag being the symbol of St John the Baptist.

Jude and Arabella go to Aldbrickham and stay at an inn near the station.

The George Hotel in King Street, Reading, is noted for its fine courtyard.

Jude stood "and surveyed Chief Street stretching ahead, with its college after college, in picturesqueness unrivalled". . .

High Street, Oxford, the famous thoroughfare of the city, is known generally as 'The High'.

Jude goes to Kennetbridge in search of a composer who is organist at the parish church.

The parish church of St Nicholas, Newbury, is a fine example of the early 16th century. The town stands on the River Kennet.

Jude arrives at Shaston, "entering on the summit of the peak after a toilsome climb,". . .

Shaftesbury, where the picturesque and well-known Gold Hill is one of the steep ascents into the town. 'Shaston' was the contraction used on milestones for 'Shaftesbury'.

Sue and Richard Phillotson's school is in Bimport Street. "In front of the schools, which were extensive and stone-built, grew two enormous beeches". . .

Bimport is a street leading westwards from the town centre, and beech trees still remain along the Abbey Walk frontage of the old school buildings.

Waiting for lessons to finish, Jude "withdrew a few steps along Abbey Walk,". . .

Abbey Walk leads from Bimport, Shaftesbury, to the site of the former abbey.

He then "walked down to the level terrace where the Abbey gardens once had spread,". . .

Shaftesbury Abbey was founded by King Alfred (871–901) and became the wealthiest Benedictine nunnery in England.

Sue says: "We don't live at the school, you know, but in that ancient dwelling across the way called Old-Grove Place."

The Ox House, on the north side of Bimport, Shaftesbury, was built c1600 and extensively altered in 1965.

Jude misses his coach which leaves from the Duke's Arms in the Market Place.

The Grosvenor Hotel, Shaftesbury, is a fine old coaching inn dating from c1800. The head of the Grosvenor family is the Duke of Westminster. The family used to own most of the town.

Whilst waiting for the next coach, he walked through "the venerable grave-yard of Trinity Church, with its avenues of limes,". . .

Holy Trinity church, Shaftesbury, was totally rebuilt in 1841–42, the architect being Sir Gilbert Scott. Having become redundant, it has been imaginatively converted into the Trinity Centre.

Walking from Shaston to Leddenton, Richard Phillotson passes Duncliffe Hill.

Duncliffe Hill is a prominent landmark in the Stour valley west of Shaftesbury.

He visits his old friend and fellow schoolmaster George Gillingham at his school at Leddenton.

The old school building at Gillingham still remains to form part of the primary school.

Jude and Sue, both now divorcees, are living together at Aldbrickham, where they attend a wedding at the parish church.

The parish church of St Lawrence at Reading is of Norman origin with 13th and 15th century additions.

They visit the Great Wessex Agricultural Show at Stoke-Barehills, a town having a "gaunt, unattractive, ancient church,". . .

The parish church of St Michael, Basingstoke, is mostly of 15th and early 16th century date, but it has been drastically restored.

"The most familiar object in Stoke-Barehills nowadays is its cemetery, standing among some picturesque medi-aeval ruins beside the railway. . ."

The ruins on Chapel Hill in the cemetery at Basingstoke comprise the 13th and 15th century Holy Ghost Chapel and a guild chapel of 1524.

Arabella and Anny arrive in Kennet-bridge and stay at a temperance hotel, although Anny "would sooner have put up at the Chequers or the Jack".

The Chequers Hotel, Newbury. A former inn, The Jack is now a shop, having a 16th century oriel window on the first floor. Newbury is on the Kennet and Avon Canal.

Arabella has come to Kennetbridge to attend the foundation stone laying ceremony of a new chapel.

The Baptist Chapel at Newbury was built in 1859 at Northbrook Street, but was later rebuilt on its present site at St Mary's Hill.

Jude and Sue return to Christminster. "They turned in on the left by the church with the Italian porch, whose helical columns were heavily draped with creepers. . ."

The church of St Mary-the-Virgin, Oxford, the porch of which has distinctive spiral columns.

Lodgings for Sue and the children are eventually found in a Christminster back street near Sarcophagus College.

Corpus Christi College, Oxford, was founded in 1516.

From her lodgings, Sue can also see the outlines of Rubric College.

Brasenose College, Oxford, was founded in 1509.

Arabella, returning from Marygreen to Alfredston, approaches "the old alms-houses in the first street of the town".

Stile's Almshouses in Newbury Street, Wantage, were built in 1680.

When Sue returns to Richard Phillotson at Marygreen, she hires a conveyance at The Bear in Alfredston.

Jude dies whilst Arabella is attending the Remembrance Day festivities in the city. At one point "She entered under the archway of Oldgate College,". . .

The early 19th century Bear Hotel at Wantage is situated in the Market Place.

New College, Oxford, was founded in 1379.

The 15th century King's House in The Close at Salisbury, Wiltshire.

The Grosvenor Hotel in The Commons at Shaftesbury.

Holy Ghost chapel ruins, in the cemetery at Basingstoke, Hampshire.

Jude the Obscure

39.   A Committee Man of 'The Terror'

THE SCENE is Budmouth in the years 1802–03; two French nationals are lodging in the town – a young aristocratic lady whose family were executed during the French Revolution, and a prominent member of the revolutionary committee who had been instrumental in bringing them to the guillotine. The renewal of hostilities between England and France brings them together as fellow aliens, and in spite of the lady's initial repugnance of the man, they plan to marry and leave the country.

King George III and the royal family are staying for the season in "our old-fashioned watering-place," and the town is thronged with visitors.

Weymouth in 1802–03, a location and period similar to that of *The Trumpet Major*.

A Frenchman arrives in the town and "moved onward down St. Thomas Street, and approached the bridge over the harbour backwater,"...

Between 1770 and 1824 Weymouth Harbour was spanned by a timber bridge opposite St. Nicholas Street, some way to the west of the present bridge.

The Frenchman crossed the harbour bridge and went to "the Old Rooms Inn, where he engaged a bedchamber".

The Old Rooms in Trinity Street is an Elizabethan house which was used as assembly rooms in the 18th century.

The French lady lives in the other part of the town on the north side of the harbour, but she often sees the Frenchman on the other side. On one occasion "he was standing by Cove Row, on the quay opposite".

Cove Row, Weymouth, is a terrace of cottages built c1808 on land reclaimed from the harbour where there had formerly been a more cove-like feature. The cottages would not therefore have existed in 1803.

On another occasion they meet at the theatre.

The former Theatre Royal at Weymouth (see *The Trumpet Major*).

The Frenchman stands meditatively looking out to sea on "the Lookout Hill,"...

The Nothe, Weymouth, a gun emplacement since the 17th century, was built as a fort 1860–72.

The Frenchman's more permanent lodgings are "over a shop, halfway up the steep and narrow street of the old town,"...

High Street, Weymouth, on the south side of the harbour. Much of it has disappeared due to wartime bombing and redevelopment, but a section remains at the west end near Boot Hill.

The French lady decides to flee to London, but changes her mind and returns when the coach reaches the White Hart at Melchester.

The White Hart Hotel in St John's Street, Salisbury, is a late 18th century coaching inn with an imposing Ionic portico.

40. The Duke's Reappearance

IN JULY 1685 the Duke of Monmouth, illegitimate son of King Charles II (1660-1685), landed at Lyme Regis with the aim of raising an army in the west country, and claiming the throne from his uncle, King James II (1685-1688). However, his claim was short-lived, for his badly trained army was soon defeated at the battle of Sedgemoor, and the Duke himself fled, being captured a few days later at Monmouth's Ash near Horton. He was subsequently executed, and a great number of his supporters were rounded up and tried at the Bloody Assizes under the notorious Judge Jeffreys. This short story is based on a supposed legend that the Duke took refuge for a short while after his defeat in a lonely cottage at King's Hintock (Melbury Osmund).

Christopher Swetman lives in a house with mullioned windows "on the outskirts of King's-Hintock village," . . . Here a stranger arrives asking for shelter.

A 17th century stone and thatched cottage at the south end of Melbury Osmund is now known as Monmouth Cottage. (Hardy's mother, Jemima Hand, came from Melbury Osmund.)

Rumours had already reached King's-Hintock that "the rightful King of England had landed . . . at a port only eighteen miles to the south-west". . .

Lyme Regis, in the extreme south west of Dorset, is not otherwise referred to by Hardy, although it was made famous by Jane Austen (1775-1817).

Making himself useful, the stranger fetches water "from Buttock's Spring in the dip near the house". . .

Not far from Monmouth Cottage, Melbury Osmond, there is a ford where a small stream crosses the road.

On leaving the cottage, the stranger "disappeared through Clammers Gate by the road that crosses King's Hintock Park to Evershead".

The entrance to Melbury Park at Town's End, near Monmouth Cottage. The drive still continues past Melbury House southwards to Evershot.

One of those killed in the recent battle was the brother of the lord of the manor "who lived at King's-Hintock Court hard by".

Melbury House (see *A Group of Noble Dames*).

Monmouth Cottage at Townsend, Melbury Osmund. The Swetman family of Melbury Osmund were ancestors of Hardy on his mother's side.

The Duke's Reappearance

41.   The Grave by the Handpost

THE PERIOD covered by this short story extends from the first decade of the 19th century (the gravestone is dated 20 December 180–) to the year of Waterloo (1815). The Chalk-Newton choir and instrumentalists are making their customary rounds of the parish performing carols on Christmas night, when they encounter men from Sidlinch burying the body of a suicide victim at the crossroads on the parish boundary where the lane between the two villages crosses Long Ash Lane.

On Christmas Eve the Chalk-Newton church band and choir assemble "by the stone stump of the cross in the middle of the village, near the White Horse Inn,". . .

The base of a mediaeval market cross still stands at Maiden Newton near the White Horse Inn. This former Elizabethan inn was rebuilt c1900, and is now closed.

The choir see lights at the crossroads between Chalk-Newton and Sidlinch, and find Sidlinch men burying the body of old Samuel Holway.

An old trackway still runs in a direct line between Maiden Newton and Sydling. It crosses the A37, or Long Ash Lane, at Break Heart Hill.

Ezra Cattstock goes to Chalk-Newton rectory to make arrangements for the body to be transferred to the churchyard.

The old rectory at Maiden Newton stands just to the south of the church, beside the Frome meadows. Cattistock is the next village to the north.

Luke Holway, Samuel's son, returns to Sidlinch after fighting victoriously at Waterloo.

Sydling St. Nicholas. In the Domesday survey of 1086 it is referred to as Sidelince.

The mediaeval cross base at Maiden Newton.

The western section of the old direct road between Maiden Newton and Sydling St. Nicholas where it meets the A37 or Long Ash Lane. This would have been the crossroads, on Break Heart Hill, which features in the story The Grave by the Handpost. The eastern section from here, to Sydling, is now a public bridleway.

42. Enter a Dragoon

THE SCENE is an isolated part of Mellstock parish, the period is that of the Crimean War (1854–56), and the dragoon is Corporal John Clark, who is called away to war just before his intended marriage to Selina Paddock.

Selina Paddock lives with her parents in a cottage which "stood at the top of a garden stretching down to the lane or street that ran through a hermit-group of dwellings in Mellstock parish".

On the tithe map of 1839, a cottage with a large front garden is shown on the north side of the lane at Higher Bockhampton, not far from the Hardy's cottage.

Corporal John Clark of the Dragoons was stationed at Casterbridge barracks at the time of his courtship with Selina.

The former Marabout barracks off Poundbury Road, Dorchester were built as cavalry barracks in 1794–95.

A list of soldiers killed at the Battle of the Alma (20 September 1854) "was nailed up against Casterbridge Town Hall door," and John Clark appears to have been among them.

The Dorchester town hall and corn exchange was rebuilt in its present form in 1847–48, with the exception of the clock turret which was added in 1863.

John Clark was not killed after all, for a letter from him has arrived. It had been "brought up from Lower Mellstock Post-Office".. .

The northernmost of a pair of cottages at Lower Bockhampton opposite the lane which leads to the old school, is marked as the post office on the 1902 Ordnance Survey map.

John Clark dies just after returning to the Paddock's house, and his funeral procession is led by a military band from Casterbridge barracks by way of the High Street "to the churchyard in the Durnover quarter".. .

The route would have been along High West Street, High East Street and Fordington High Street to Fordington church.

After the funeral, Selina "turned over Swan bridge and homeward to Mellstock".

The former brick-built Swan bridge at the bottom of High East Street was rebuilt in stone in 1954.

Selina, now regarding herself as a widow, leaves home and opens a fruit and vegetable shop at Chalk-Newton.

Maiden Newton, a village which features several times in the Wessex novels and short stories.

A pair of cottages at Lower Bockhampton, Stinsford, opposite the lane leading to the old school and Kingston Maurward. The cottage on the left was formerly the post office.

43. A Changed Man

AFTER THEIR marriage, Captain John Maumbry and his wife Laura are the most fashionable young couple in Casterbridge, but their bright lifestyle does not last long, for Captain Maumbry resigns his commission and enters the church to become a curate in the poor parish of Durnover. When a cholera outbreak occurs in the parish, Laura is evacuated to Creston whilst the Reverend Maumbry remains to attend to the sick and dying.

The character of John Maumbry is generally considered to have been based on Henry Moule, who was vicar of Fordington 1829–80, and ministered to his sick and dying parishioners during cholera epidemics in 1849 and 1854. The story is set in the latter period (after the railway from Bristol to Yeovil was constructed in 1853, and before the Yeovil to Weymouth section was opened in 1857), so that many of the locations in and around the town are the same as those featuring in *The Mayor of Casterbridge.*

An invalid observes Casterbridge life from a first floor oriel window of "a substantially-built house . . . just below Top o' Town . . . whence could be obtained a raking view of the High Street, west and east, the former including Laura's dwelling, . . . and the turning that led to the cavalry barracks". . . .

As Laura's house and the turning to the barracks could be seen, the house with the oriel window was evidently on the south side of High West Street, and from old prints and photographs it appears to have been situated where the Stings night-club now stands at 37/38 High West Street, Dorchester.

Captain Maumbry arrives with a Hussar regiment at Casterbridge barracks.

The Marabout barracks built in 1794–95 in Poundbury Road behind The Grove.

Laura lives at her uncle's house which is situated "at the corner of West Street nearest the barracks."

41 High West Street, Dorchester, stands at the corner leading to Colliton Walk alongside The Grove.

A new curate comes to "the Chapel-of-ease attended by the troops" . . . and his preaching has a considerable effect on Captain Maumbry.

Christ Church, off The Grove, Dorchester, was a new parochial chapel opened in 1846 to serve the western part of Fordington parish, and as a garrison church for the nearby barracks.

Captain Maumbry resigns his commission and goes to Fountall Theological College.

Wells Theological College (see *A Tragedy of Two Ambitions*).

The regular customers in the White Hart do not consider Maumbry's move from the army to the church to have been a wise one.

The White Hart Hotel at the bottom of High East Street, Dorchester has been rebuilt since the 19th century.

The Maumbrys now live in a humble cottage in Durnover Lane.

Probably Holloway Road, a narrow lane between Mill Street and Fordington High Street.

There is an outbreak of cholera in Durnover parish, the worst affected area being Mixen Lane.

Mill Street, Fordington, was a squalid and overcrowded area where various diseases were prevalent.

The Reverend Maumbry remains in the parish, but Laura is evacuated to Creston, on the coast near Budmouth.

Preston near Weymouth was formerly a small village, but it has now grown considerably as a holiday centre.

Laura gets to know Lieutenant Vannicock who is stationed at Budmouth infantry barracks.

The former Weymouth barracks near Hope Square now form part of a housing development known as Wellington Court.

John and Laura Maumbry meet twice a week on the Ridgeway, keeping a wall between them to minimise the risk of infection. "Walls formed the field-fences here."

The former direct route over Ridgeway Hill was abandoned in 1824 in favour of the present hairpin detour. The old track still remains between dry-stone wall field boundaries.

Later Laura meets Lieutenant Vannicock near the same spot at "the milestone that stands on the north slope of the ridge, where the old and new roads diverge,". . .

A point on the Dorchester side of Ridgeway Hill near the Came Down and Broadmayne turning. The old milestone is no longer there, having been removed during the Second World War.

Laura and Leiutenant Vannicock plan to go away together to Ivell and thence by train to Bristol. He has a fly waiting on Mellstock Hill "to take them by a cross-cut into the Ivell Road,". . .

From Stinsford Hill there is a byroad which runs direct to the Yeovil road by way of Frome Whitfield and Charminster.

On nearing Casterbridge they turn "to the right at the Roman Amphitheatre" . . . and arrive at Durnover Cross.

A right turn at Maumbury Rings, at what would have been the southern outskirts of Dorchester in Victorian times, leads by way of Maumbury Road, Maumbury Way (now Monmouth Road) and King's Road to Fordington Cross.

"By Standfast Corner, a little beyond the Cross, they suddenly obtained an end view of the lane." (Mixen Lane.)

The junction where Mill Lane joins Kings Road at Prince's Bridge just to the north of Fordington Cross.

High West Street, Dorchester, from Top o' Town. A photolithograph from John Pouncy's Dorset Photographically Illustrated (1857). A building with a first floor oriel window can be seen a little way down the street on the right.

A Changed Man

44. Old Mrs Chundle

THIS SHORT story, although written c1888–90, was not published until after Hardy's death, when it appeared in the Ladies' Home Journal of February 1929. It is said to have been based on a true story related by Henry J. Moule who was curator of the Dorset County Museum and a talented watercolourist.

The curate of Kingscreech persuades a deaf old lady, Mrs Chundle, to attend his church, and arranges for a speaking-tube to be fitted on the pulpit so that she can sit close underneath and hear his sermons. 'Kingscreech' is obviously an amalgamation of Kingston and Creech, and although generally held to represent Kingston, this seems unlikely on at least two counts. Firstly, Kingston is referred to as Little Enckworth in *The Hand of Ethelberta*, and secondly a reference to Creechbarrow in the story suggests that Kingscreech church is the nearby one at Creech rather than that at Kingston which is some three miles distant from Creechbarrow. In addition, Mrs Chundle's cottage is said to lie three miles from Enckworth Court (Encombe House).

The curate of Kingscreech is in an outlying part of his parish, near Mrs Chundle's cottage, painting "a distant view of the Corvsgate ruin two miles off.", . . .

Furzebrook is two miles from Corfe Castle, and about three miles from Encombe, although it lies in Church Knowle parish rather than Steeple in which Creech is situated.

The curate persuades the deaf Mrs Chundle to attend his church.

Creech church was first built in 1746 incorporating the chancel arch and other Norman details from the ruins of Holme Priory.

An ear-trumpet provided for Mrs Chundle proves ineffective – "You might as well have been mouthing at me from the top o' Creech Barrow."

Creechbarrow, Dorset's miniature mountain, although at 634 feet not the highest point in the Isle of Purbeck, is the most prominent and distinctive feature.

'Creech Barrow from the Wareham Road', drawn by Alfred Dawson in 1882.
Source: Rodney Legg collection.

Index